First published in Great Britain in 2019 by
iNostalgia Ltd, Progress Centre, Charlton
Place, Ardwick, Manchester, M12 6HS,

Photography © 2019:
Emma Finch, Sue Anders, Nigel Kingston,
Karen Wright, Bernadette Delaney,
People's History Museum, Andrew Simcock,
Ian 'Tom' Tomie and Crown Copyright

Illustrations commissioned in creative
partnership with Women in Print © 2019:
Sneaky Raccoon, Deanna Halsall,
Helen Musselwhite, Laura Boast, Nell Smith,
Artsynibs, Amy Rodchester, Eve Warren,
Ellie Thomas, Emma Bowen, Maisy Summer,
Tomekah George, Alex Francis, Laura Bohill,
Halah El-Kholy, Wendy Wong, Chelsea Waites,
Nicola Fernandes, Emily Dayson
and Sarah Wilson

Cover Design © Jane Bowyer 2019

Text © 2019 Helen Antrobus
Text © 2019 Andrew Simcock

Helen Antrobus and Andrew Simcock have
asserted their rights to be identified as the
authors of this work in accordance with the
Copyright, Designs and Patents Act 1988.

Design: Matt Lamont (Foxduo Design Ltd)

Edit: Emily Wright

ISBN 978-1-84547-252-8

This book is for Emily Stott – not the first in the fight, but its future

Dedicated to the memory of Ursula 'Uschi' Iredale, 1954 - 2019

FIRST · IN
THE · FIGHT

BY

HELEN ANTROBUS
&
ANDREW SIMCOCK

iNostalgia
Publishing

'Where are all the women?'

Over the past five years, a mass of building and roadworks overtook the city of Manchester, changing it, in some parts unrecognisably, from the city it would have been in 1918. Roads have been re-routed, buildings demolished; and yet, when looking back at the black and white photographs of the city from over a hundred years ago, the familiarity of those tall, majestic buildings, the smoke in the air and the busy, hustling streets, is unmistakable. What is not lost from the physical changes is the character of the place. A city of industry, miles away both geographically and culturally from the capital of London. To paraphrase Tony Wilson, this is Manchester. Things are done differently here.

Manchester was a city borne of hard work and innovation, from both the industrial revolution that placed it at the centre of European trade, and the radicalisation of its people and politics. On 4th December 1918, the first women to be legally able to vote walked to the polling stations for the very first time, after a fierce, exhausting battle, the roots of which were buried in the streets of Manchester.

The emotions that must have channelled through the city that day would have been incredible; victory, elation and perhaps some scepticism. There would have been grief too, as the day would have been overshadowed by the massive loss of life during the First World War, that had come to an end only a month earlier. The memory of the men who would never vote again, and the women who would never have the opportunity, must surely have darkened the day.

One hundred years later, on a freezing cold winter's day, identical emotions filled the city of Manchester and the air filled with purple, white, and green. Oxford Road, the route between St Peter's Square and Nelson Street, was alive with the same colours, placards, rosettes, chants and songs. The time had come, a century since some women could first vote, to unveil the statue of Emmeline Pankhurst in the centre of the city. Hard work and dedication had brought Manchester to this moment, as people from all over joined in the celebration.

Whilst the statue of Emmeline Pankhurst was at the heart of these celebrations, the day represented a year-long commemoration of the 1918 Representation of the People Act. It was a year of national significance; a year for many to look back, reflect, question and challenge how much has changed today. Whilst victory and elation stood shoulder to shoulder in St Peter's Square, there was no doubt that there was something bittersweet about the celebration. For many women, their lives would not have been so different long ago, and there is still much left to do in the fight for equality.

The Sculpture Hall in Manchester Town Hall was where Andrew Simcock's story of the statue campaign began, in the spring of 2014. Whilst meeting with a friend, she cast an eye around the dimly-lit, Victorian space, and said to him: 'These are all men – where are all the women?'

When this invisibility isn't called to question, it is difficult to see. Perhaps some of the civil servants, councillors and visitors may have pondered this quietly as they walked through the hall; perhaps there had already been half-formed, forgotten conversations about the potential for a female statue in the city. Only recently, the portrait of Margaret Ashton, Manchester's first female councillor, had been re-hung in the Town Hall after it had been rejected by male councillors due to her stance on the First World War, and, most probably, the widely-accepted misogynistic tendencies towards female politicians that filled political spaces in the early 20th century. This may have inspired some conversations about what else could be done about these hidden figures, but no action was taken. The Town Hall and the city it stood in remained free of female memorials, save one: an impressively dour, over-sized statue of Queen Victoria, which was, and is, almost permanently covered in bird excrement.

In 2014 Jenny White and Helen Davies carried out the Stature Project, yarn-bombing the male busts in the Sculpture Hall with the faces of women who had shaped the history of Manchester. Seeing this bold and artistic intervention demonstrated even further how much a statue of a woman in the city would be appreciated.

These two events in the Sculpture Hall were to lead, almost five years later, to the unveiling of the statue of Emmeline Pankhurst in front of over six thousand people on a cold, bright December morning.

Emmeline was the first statue of a woman to be erected in Manchester since 1901. The first statue remains today in Piccadilly Gardens, where, in 1908, Manchester suffragettes Annot Robinson and Mabel Capper were prohibited by the police from advertising their next meeting at the foot of it. It seems both surprising and unsurprising that they would choose Queen Victoria as a base for their campaigning; whilst she represented the sound argument that a woman could confidently and capably take centre stage in political affairs, Victoria famously spoke out against those who argued for women's suffrage. Still, it is entirely understandable why Mabel and Annot chose that spot; to rally at a memorial to a powerful woman was symbolic of what they, if given the opportunity, could achieve.

The statue of Victoria, however, had a chequered past. Over a thousand people had lined the streets of Manchester to see the statue unveiled by Lord Roberts. Whilst the procession was popular amongst the crowds, the speeches given by a selection of politicians and aristocracy could only be witnessed by an invited handful of guests, who had been given a spot at the front of the statue. The crowd grew restless. It was reported in the Manchester Guardian that:

'There were many violent rushes towards the statue, and again and again the lines of volunteers and police were broken… real order was never restored, and there were frequent cases of fainting and collapse.'

Whilst the unveiling of both statues, save the frustrations and violence of the crowd in 1901, were both viewed as overwhelmingly successful events, the reactions to the statue of Victoria make it increasingly evident why Emmeline is so important. There's no denying that she's far from perfect – who in history is? – but she does offer something that the statue of Victoria does not.

Since the statue of Emmeline has been unveiled, it has remained both an attraction and a meeting point for residents and tourists alike. Flowers are left weekly at the foot of the statue; sometimes, when walking through St Peter's Square past the winding yellow trams and the purple paulownia trees, a small bouquet can be seen neatly tucked into Emmeline's bronze, outstretched hand. Whilst Victoria, over a century on, sits as a faded symbol of empire and patriotism in Piccadilly Gardens, oversized and feet above the commuters bustling to Piccadilly train station, Emmeline represents something entirely different. She is Mancunian. The streets of this city meant something to her, other than what they meant to the nation's industry; it was home. The organisation that she devoted her life and health to was founded in the parlour of her home, 61 Nelson Street. She spoke on platforms in Heaton Park, and in the Free Trade Hall. This city is her city. To see her, across the Square from Manchester Town Hall, is a reminder of what women from Manchester are capable of.

Andrew Simcock's journey to procuring the statue of Emmeline Pankhurst is nestled amongst the fleeting (and they are fleeting) snapshots of the twenty women who were long-listed for the honour. It is a story of determination and commitment to the city's long, campaigning history. Andrew's fundraising work for the statue involved everything from a gruelling cycle ride from Lands End to John O Groats, to working with corporate partners and sponsorship, and securing government funding in the year of the centenary. It is thanks to those efforts that the statue stands today.

But what if this had all been at a different place, in a different time? I find it a slightly troubling question, one that I would stop myself from asking, telling myself it is too much playing devil's advocate to ask, that it no longer matters. But I fear I know the answer to it, and the answer, as always, feels more disappointing than asking the question in the first place. Despite a campaign that, I'm certain, would have funded a statue at some point, would this statue have been commissioned, funded and stand now, proudly in St Peter's Square, if not for the centenary of some women first being granted the vote?

It is doubtful. This should not detract from the determination of the campaign – even if it had happened in ten or twenty years, there were long-term fundraising plans for a statue of a woman in the city centre. However, the funding received from the government accelerated this process, so it was unveiled in 2018.

For those who have made the women's suffrage movement and the lives of those who led it their life's work, the centenary was a moment of both great celebration and frustration. Half-researched stories of the Pankhurst family began to spread across the internet, whilst television programmes seemed to mislabel every woman who campaigned for enfranchisement as a suffragette, not recognising the nuances of the different campaigning groups and organisations. For the most past, it was a celebration of a handful of 'heroines' and the result of a long, arduous campaign. The complexities of these women, their mistakes, their flaws, and their achievements beyond this one moment in time, were lost. Broader discussions of representation were mishandled. People so readily agreed that they too would have been a suffragette one hundred years ago without stopping to consider the mental and physical torture of gaol and force-feeding. Polarising these excited opinions were the outrage at celebrating historic 'terrorists' who bombed public spaces and attacked innocent people. Indeed, the centenary unearthed a new wave of deep-rooted misogyny across the UK, when women's history, for perhaps the first time, was brought to the forefront of national celebration and public memory.

Through the government funding scheme that would help to fund the Emmeline Pankhurst statue, national and local commemorations were held across the country. From marches, artworks, and public memorials to prime-time television programmes, it truly was the year of the woman, and the campaigning woman at that. Women who were beaten, women who were force-fed, women who were silenced were recognised as heroes, and uncomfortable comparisons of gender inequality, violence against women, and the treatment of migrant women, were thrown into public light, to be questioned, to be de-constructed.

The debate that raged through these commemorations, that tore through the revelry like a stone shattering a window, was clear: how far have we really come in a hundred years?

Amongst all of this, it seemed everybody was looking to Manchester, the symbolic birthplace of the movement, to see what it would do to mark such a significant year. With years of planning having led to this moment, it is unsurprising that the statue would become a public symbol of the centenary of the Representation of the People Act, recognised as perhaps one of the biggest moments in political history. Across Manchester, plans were already underway in every heritage institution, across schools and universities, charities and private businesses.

The purple, white and green of the Women's Social and Political Union (WSPU) seemed to be adopted as Manchester's new emblem. 'Deeds Not Words' carried more weight and more relevance than 'Concilio Et Labore', the words on Manchester's coat of arms. The statue of Emmeline Pankhurst not only became a symbol of the centenary, but of local pride, national importance, and a moment of recognition for the women who made Manchester.

There are, of course, questions raised about the co-creation and public investment in the statue. The long-list, as Andrew explains, came from a number of suggestions from colleagues and members of the public, who took an interest in the statue campaign. But the list by no means represents women from across the city, and in between the stories of the women who were on the list, it is necessary to focus on those who weren't, bringing into question perhaps the lack of community involvement in the long-listing process. Indeed, even the WoManchester statue selection committee had a lack of community representation. It is perhaps fair to raise: how much of Manchester were actually part of WoManchester?

The answer lies in the public voting, which took place once the shortlist of women was revised. Across regional news programmes and articles, each woman was advocated for and a plea went out to vote for her. A common phrase began to sound as these advocacies aired: 'Why can't we have statues of all of these women?' The shortlisted women all resonated for different reasons. They represent, amongst other things, culture, entrepreneurship, the radical roots of the city, the birth of the suffragettes and equality in a broad and sweeping concept.

Those six women were:

Elizabeth Gaskell

Elizabeth Raffald

Ellen Wilkinson

Margaret Ashton

Emmeline Pankhurst

Louise Da-Cocodia

Emmeline Pankhurst won the public vote by a landslide. This doesn't feel like a surprise – of all the names on the list, hers is the most well-known and celebrated across the city. But Manchester is not a one-woman city. The tenacity and the fight that brewed at the heart of Emmeline Pankhurst was not exclusive. Before and after her lived women of exceptional strength and vision, who defied expectations, misogyny, and social prejudice. These are the women who changed our education, our health care, our birth control, our rights to vote; women who became entrepreneurs and visionaries. The statue of Emmeline represents these revolutionary women; those who she would stand on the shoulders of, and those who would stand on her own.

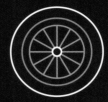

The selection of twenty women has both light and shade. The age-old issue of diversity has to be brought into question here. It doesn't showcase the powerful, and rich LGBT+ stories, nor a particularly wide selection of the BAME narratives that have shaped the city of Manchester. It raises the question: are these stories perpetually 'hidden' from our histories? As Emmeline Pankhurst and fellow suffragists and suffragettes fought for representation, should we now be picking up the mantle, and using campaigns of memorialisation, commemoration and national recognition such as the statue campaign, to highlight these serious issues?

It's food for thought.

What these women and this campaign offers, however, is an overwhelming sense of hope. The hope that long struggles and short struggles, ambitions that seem unachievable, doors slammed suddenly don't look like an ending – just stumbling blocks.

Each of these women deserves a statue, but there could only be one. This book, in its own small way, will shine some light on the nineteen other women who could have been commemorated in St Peter's Square, and the thousands of incredible, powerful women across Manchester, past and present.

Bring Out The Banners: Manchester's Radical Past

It was cotton that did it. Cotton that had travelled across continents and seas, from the hands of workers and slaves across the world. Manchester was the centre of the textile trade, producing over thirty percent of the world's cotton. First water-powered, then steam-powered, the mills of Manchester were the life-blood of the city. Women dominated this workforce and by the early 20th century, every mill town in Lancashire was filled with women workers. It was cotton that put Manchester on the world map – and women were the force behind the cotton.

The cotton industry radicalised the city towards a movement that changed the political face of the country. Workers began to unionise and demand suffrage, fight for reform, against corruption and for better working conditions. It culminated, at first, with the Peterloo Massacre, where tens of thousands gathered on St Peter's field to campaign for reform. The magistrates ordered in the yeomanry and the hussars to disperse the crowd and what had been an act of peaceful protest descended into chaos and violence. The legacy of the Peterloo Massacre is deep-rooted in Manchester. Even though it is not recognised nationally as

perhaps it should be, here in Manchester it is understood as the root of radicalism in this city. Manchester was radical before the suffragettes and it will carry on being so.

In this section we explore the women who were integral to the radical roots of the city of Manchester. They were in the crowds at Peterloo, on the hustings alongside Henry Hunt and part of the Chartist agitation that swept through the country. Women formed their own societies and meetings, becoming political commentators and educators in their own right. **Margaret Downes** represents the women of Peterloo. **Margaret Ashton** was the first female councillor in Manchester and was, amongst other things, a campaigner for women's suffrage, trade unions, and female education. **Esther Roper** helped found the Lancashire and Cheshire Women's Textile Workers Committee, fighting for fair representation for women workers, while **Mary Quaile** similarly worked relentlessly to ensure fair representation for women within the trade unions. **Ellen Wilkinson**, one of the first female Members of Parliament, similarly used her voice to champion peace, universal suffrage, women in trade unions, higher education and rallied against poverty and war. All of these

women represent the intersectional political mindsets that women had at the time, dismissing the idea that it was suffrage, and suffrage alone, that radicalised women. They sit in a long line of female political campaigners, who fought not only for the rights of their own sex, but for universal justice, liberty and equality.

The banners and ephemera left behind by these women do not sit alone in the museums and archives of Manchester. Over the last one hundred years, protest materials from banners and placards, to badges and items of clothing, have been collected and archived. From 'Reclaim the Night' to strikes for equal pay, LGBT+ marches and the now infamous Women's March against the inauguration of Donald Trump, these items show that, whilst the fight may be different, it still carries on. The women of Manchester still readily dive head-first into the fight for equality, justice, peace, and liberty.

MARGARET DOWNES

There was music playing as the crowds poured into St Peter's Fields on 16th August 1819. It was summer; the day would have been clear and warm. The people who gathered were dressed in their best clothes; many of the women wore gowns of white, their bonnets tied with ribbons. Accompanied by the bands from Middleton, people from all over Manchester walked to where hustings had been built in front of Windmill Street. Flags and banners were flown, their colours vivid against the blue sky.

Amongst all of this, the magistrates gathered in Mr Edward Buxton's house on Mount Street, watching and waiting.

Earlier that week, notices had been posted for a gathering, but it had been cancelled when the magistrates had made it clear that any caught would be arrested, though no law was to be broken. *Fear God and Honour the King*, the print had read in heavy, black typeface. This did not deter the Manchester Patriotic Union, and the swells of reformers in the city; something in Manchester needed to change and action could only have been brought about by the many, not the few.

Manchester, which was fast becoming an international hub of trade and textiles with the mills on the edge of the city booming with prosperity and production, still did not have fair political representation in the House of Commons; only two Members of Parliament represented the entire county of Lancashire. As an industrial town, the new-found riches came hand in hand with poverty; slums covered the city, with many workers living in appalling conditions.

In July 1819, the Manchester Patriotic Union invited radical reformer Henry 'Orator' Hunt to speak at a public meeting. Hunt, a gentleman farmer-turned-radical, accepted. He was a natural performer, known for his incredible public meetings and his love of cheer from the crowd. Hunt came to speak out against the Corn Laws, which kept the price of wheat artificially high, but before his speech had barely begun, the magistrates ordered his arrest. Moments later, chaos broke out; as the Riot Act was read, the peaceful crowd that gathered that day was dispersed by the Hussars and the Yeomanry on horseback, with sabres. Approximately eighteen people were killed. Thousands were injured. There was never any retribution; Hunt was sent to prison, alongside many of the protesters. The chief constable, Joseph Nadin, was commended for his ruthless actions on the day, and all talk of revolution and change was silenced.

These events at St Peter's Fields happened almost a century before the Representation of the People Act was passed in 1918, giving some women and all men the vote - a step towards universal suffrage that so many of the campaigners that day craved. Whilst some women were actively campaigning for the vote for themselves, the women present on St Peter's Fields were not there to ask for women's suffrage, but for more men to access the ballot.

The aftermath of the massacre was stoked up into an international media storm; reports of the event reached as far as Boston, USA. Depictions made it into every publication; in most, the powerful figure of Mary Fildes, a leader amongst the female reformers and taking pride of place next to Henry Hunt on the

Illustration by **Tomekah George**

hustings, is visible in her white dress. The known satirist George Cruikshank, who had previously produced works damning the reformist societies, created a piece depicting a fallen woman, slashed across the breast, knocked to the ground, a child by her side asking for the yeomanry to stop. Eye-witness and reformer, Samuel Bamford, described a similar scene in his book, *Passage in the Life of a Radical*, saying he saw:

'A heroine, a young married woman of our party, with her face all bloody, her hair streaming about her, her bonnet hanging by the string, and her apron weighted with stones, kept her assailant at bay until she fell backwards and was near being taken…'

The woman is nameless, as many of those injured at Peterloo were. Reports from the day speak of wounded, weary and horror-struck people winding their way back down the Rochdale and Liverpool roads, heading back to the towns from which they had marched.

And so, we come to Margaret Downes – simply a name upon a list of those who died on 16th August upon St Peter's Fields. She is, perhaps, the strangest choice for the statue nomination. There were women present at the Peterloo Massacre about whom we know a great deal more; Mary Fildes, president of the Manchester Female Reformist Society and Elizabeth Gaunt or Sarah Hargreaves, both of whom were arrested and detained alongside Henry Hunt, for example. Elizabeth Gaunt, who had

been 'cut and trampled on the field', was arrested after hiding in Hunt's carriage from the fray. She was heavily pregnant and suffered a miscarriage after her arrest and imprisonment and her unborn child is now listed as one of the victims of the massacre. Even a collective depiction of the Manchester Female Reformist Society would have, perhaps, been a more obvious choice; we know from first-hand accounts and caricatures how their meetings would have been conducted.

Maragaret Downes' anonymity leaves her open to speculation as to why she had gone to St Peter's Field that day. We do not know Margaret's age. We do not know her occupation. She could have been a fervent campaigner for reform, demanding universal suffrage for men aged twenty-one and over, demanding secret ballots and annual parliaments. She could have travelled in from one of the surrounding towns or lived in the heart of the city. She could have attended the gathering with her family, like the woman in Cruikshank's cartoon, and died in front of her children. She could have gone alone, getting swept up in the crowds and been unable to escape when the yeomanry rushed in.

St Peter's Field was not women's first foray into the demand for reform and universal suffrage. Samuel Bamford, the radical reformer and eye-witness at Peterloo, noted that many women attended public meetings in the build-up. In Manchester, Stockport and Blackburn, these societies flourished. Published only days before the events on St Peter's Fields, a satirical cartoon was released of the Blackburn women reformers. Stood on their hustings, the women were depicted as overweight, pockmarked, wearing makeshift breeches and abandoning their children. A group of men ogle them from the hustings; one holds a banner pole between his legs, a cap of liberty balanced on the top. It is a crude gesture, one that paints the women as debauched, licentious and unfeminine. It was a common interpretation of political women, seen before in attacks on prominent female figures such as the Duchess of Devonshire and Mary Wollstonecraft. When stepping outside of their traditional, familial roles of mother or wife, something was breached. A woman had degraded herself, attempted to rise above what life had intended for her, and deserved to be shamed and punished for it.

It explains why the women present at Peterloo, particularly those who were committee members and dedicated to the women's reformist societies, wore white that day – symbols of purity and virtue. It would be a tactic adopted in the early 20th century, by suffragists campaigning for votes for women.

Margaret did not stand on platforms, like Mary Fildes, instead, she represents the greatest tragedy of Peterloo; innocent people, breaking no law, doing no wrong, and dying in the name of oppression. She was not alone.

There is something of a mystery to Margaret's story. Like the other victims, her death was recorded, and in one of the many pamphlets that was printed in the aftermath, Margaret's fate is listed alongside the inquest into the death of John Lees, a veteran of Waterloo who was killed on St Peter's Field. It reads:

'Margaret Downes – dreadfully cut in the breast – has been secreted clandestinely away, and cannot be heard of, supposed to be dead.'

Why was Margaret so fearfully spirited away? And who took her? Was it her family, her friends, or comrades-in-arms? Was it fear of retribution, or arrest? Many of the families of other victims were given compensation of up to £5 for the deaths of their relatives. She was only presumed dead – given the extent of her injuries described, this seems highly likely. But we will never know why she was taken away so 'clandestinely'. Perhaps her family and loved ones could not engage in the public-facing tragedy, and demand justice, whilst dealing with their own personal loss.

Margaret never did get justice. Nobody was prosecuted for what happened that day. But if a statue had stood of her in St Peter's Square, the site of that bloody, brutal, and horrifying tragedy, it would have acted as a grave reminder of what suffrage and social change would have cost in the past. Peterloo sparked a

huge shift in political thinking and reform, but it would not be until over a century later that universal suffrage was achieved. It did give rise to further reform movements such as the Chartists, and later, the suffragists and suffragettes who would dominate the demand for the vote. Margaret's death, and indeed all of those who died that day, did not mean little to those who continue their fray. They merely picked up the banner that had fallen amongst Margaret and her comrades and continued the fight for them.

MARGARET ASHTON

The struggle for women's equality and the right to hold political power was not restricted to the fight for the vote. Before 1903, when the Women's Social and Political Union (WSPU) was founded, many prolific women were championing this struggle across Manchester and the constituency of Lancashire. Amongst the women leading this fight, Margaret Ashton was at the forefront. Margaret, who was born in Manchester on 19th January 1856, was committed to these causes and spent her life campaigning for them. Once, Margaret's name would have been known nationally for the social changes she campaigned for. However, her name was all but erased after a dispute with the city council, an injustice that historians and contemporary campaigners are looking to reverse.

Margaret was born in Withington, at that time in Lancashire, in 1856. Manchester and Lancashire had flourished through industry over the previous century, and the suburb of Withington housed the affluent middle and upper classes of the city. Cotton was g cotton, whilst the merchants and companies in the centre of Manchester traded it. Margaret's father, Thomas Ashton, was a wealthy cotton manufacturer, who had started his textile company in Hyde.

Margaret was raised as a witness to her father's progressive views, and evidently, they impacted on her own political and social views (although Margaret's sister was an outspoken anti-suffragist). In 1870, when Margaret was fourteen, her father raised over £200,000 for Owens College.

The college was founded by Robert Owens to provide universal education for all, not just the privileged. Margaret's family were dedicated to the education of the poor – she taught at a school built for the children of the mill workers in Lancashire. This led to her joining three educational committees and began her campaign for women in the country.

The mills of Manchester and Lancashire were populated by women. Female textile workers were often paid a lower wage with more complicated working conditions; they had no means of challenging this as they were dissuaded from joining or forming trade unions. The life of the working-class woman was hard. Not only were they expected to run the household, raise their children and manage the household budget but many of these women also had to work long shifts in the factories. Margaret helped found the first women's local trades council in order to support these women. Working with Catherine Chisolm, Margaret backed the establishment of the first maternity hospitals in the city in 1914, supporting the needs of women who so often could not afford such treatment.

In 1900, eighteen years before the first women would be given the right to vote, Margaret became the first woman to be voted onto Withington District City Council, foreshadowing her election to Manchester City Council in 1908. For the first time, the women of Manchester were fairly represented and Margaret kept the advancement, health, education and equality of women at the heart of all she did within the community. Her role was informed by, and helped to enforce, the work she had been doing to support working women.

Illustration by **Emma Bowen**

Throughout her life and reflected in all she did, was the importance of the principles that Margaret stood and lived by. Her commitment to equality and peace wholly informed the life she led, and often resulted in her breaking away from things that she had earlier committed her support and her voice to. Despite being an avid member of the Liberal Party, Margaret resigned from the party when they refused to support a cause that meant more to Margaret than almost any other: women's suffrage.

Whilst many of her other causes were informed by her family, Margaret's reformist upbringing stopped short at women's equality. For a woman of Margaret's background and status, she was expected to invest her time and energy into charity and mission work. Despite her clear intelligence and her drive, Margaret's father refused to let her be part of the family business. This may have been the driving force for Margaret's involvement in the campaign for women's suffrage. Her work with other women's organisations led her to joining – and helping to lead – the Manchester Society for Women's Suffrage, as part of the National Union of Women's Suffrage Societies.

Margaret's notoriety became apparent when she was invited to be part of the deputation on May 19th 1906 to ask the Liberal government, under the leadership of Henry Campbell-Bannerman, to give women the vote. Although he refused, it marked an incredibly unifying moment in the campaign for women's suffrage, as working-class women, upper-class women, peaceful women and militants came together. The deputation represented over a thousand signatories from over twenty different organisations, including the Manchester and Salford Women's Trade and Labour Council, and the Women's Liberal Federation. During her time with the NUWSS, Margaret was the leading funder and contributor to the pro-suffrage newspaper, *The Common Cause*.

The differences between the methods used by the suffrage campaigners would often fracture these groups from each other. It would not have come as a surprise that Margaret signed a public letter condemning the actions of the militant Women's Social and Political Union (WSPU). Pacifism had been ingrained into Margaret, and much like the fight for women's suffrage,

would inform and direct how she lived her life. In 1914, at the outbreak of the First World War, Margaret's dedication to peace would be taken onto an international platform, campaigning with the Women's International League for Peace and Freedom (WILPF).

Like many other suffrage societies, the NUWSS voted in favour of the war, although they did not actively commit to the war effort as their WSPU sisters did. Margaret resigned from the organisation she had committed so many years of tireless campaigning to on account of this. However, she continued to lobby for the vote and for adult suffrage – the vote for all men and women aged 21 and over – through her other organisations.

Margaret's name resounded around Manchester, but despite having schools and buildings named after her, she failed to become one of the names that resonated in modern households and never gained the long-lasting notoriety of the Pankhursts. Why, then? Visibility plays a big part here, and in the 1920s, Manchester City Council made a decision that would affect Margaret's legacy for almost a century.

To mark her 70th birthday, Manchester Guardian editor C P Scott commissioned a portrait of Margaret to be painted. Looking stern and regal, in simple dress and unsmiling, Margaret balances the traditionally rigid Victorian fashions that she would have been born into, whilst maintaining an effortless look of modernity. It was tradition that the councillors of Manchester would have their portraits hanging in the town hall – many of which can be seen today. Margaret's portrait, however, was rejected. The councillors of Manchester, on account of the protestations against the First World War, viewed Margaret as a traitor, and she was removed from the Education Committee in 1917. Despite being the first woman in the council chamber, despite the energy, time, and change she had put into it, Margaret would not be immortalised on those walls as her peers would have been.

Perhaps if the portrait had been hung on the wall, Margaret's name would have been better known, but all is not lost. Margaret Ashton's name resurfaced in Manchester in 2006, when historian

Alison Ronan discovered references to the portrait amongst Margaret's papers, and subsequently helped to unearth the painting from the stores of Manchester Art Gallery. It has since been re-hung at Manchester Town Hall, before being displayed at both the People's History Museum and Manchester Art Gallery.

It was tradition that the councillors of Manchester would have their portraits hanging in the town hall – many of which can be seen today. Margaret's portrait, however, was rejected.

MARY QUAILE

Many of the women nominated for the Manchester statue, unsurprisingly, had a close connection to the fight for women's suffrage. There was a surplus on the list of women who had lobbied parliament and smashed windows, who had set up petitions and marched in the streets under banners of green, purple and white. The women who lived alongside these campaigners, who weren't necessarily flying the same colours, are often forgotten. One of these women is undoubtedly Mary Quaile, a feminist and trade unionist who dedicated her life to improving working conditions for working-class women. Her work led her to Russia and back, and her politics and values, though questioned at times, guided her throughout her life. She was a remarkable woman and a reminder that a strong Manchester woman needn't always be reflected back through history as a suffragette.

Mary Quaile was born in Dublin, Ireland, on 8th August 1886. When Mary was still a toddler, Mary's parents moved to Manchester from their home in Dublin, which offered industry and work to many immigrants. Historically, Irish families were treated poorly and often with bigotry in cities such as Manchester and Liverpool. Mary's father, James, was a bricklayer and played an active role in his trade union, the Ancient Guild of Incorporated Brick and Stone Layers. Based on her father's role in the union we can assume, like many other radical women, Mary was raised in a household that, whilst poor, encouraged radical thinking and supported social reform. The world was changing and families like the Quailes were changing with it.

As with many working-class families, everybody was expected to work to bring in money for the household and to pay their way. Mary left school at the age of twelve and worked firstly as a domestic servant. What role she had we don't know, but the life of a maid was tough, with long hours and little time off.

The trade union movement had grown rapidly throughout the 19th century. From the early, outlawed days of the Unlawful Oaths Act and the secret societies, the movement had grown to become one of the largest and strongest in the country.

Despite the power of the trade unions and their commitment to equality and fairness for workers, a huge amount of the trade unions, led by the Trade Union Congress (TUC) didn't support women workers. Women workers, especially in the city of Manchester, made up a huge amount of the workforce and dominated the textile industry, but most remained unorganised and underrepresented. For doing the same job as a male counterpart, women were paid less, and despite movements from women such as Clementina Black and the Women's Industrial Council, the trade union's culture and prejudice against women workers struggled to change. Women were left with lower wages, difficult working conditions and only a handful of people to speak out for them. Soon, Mary would emerge as a voice for the voiceless, as she began to embed herself in the world of trade unions.

In 1908, the Clarion Café opened on Market Street, in Manchester. *The Clarion* was a socialist newspaper founded by Robert Blatchford in 1890. The newspaper inspired a movement across the country that encouraged working-class people to pursue new leisurely and cultural activities, such as rambling and cycling. Clarion clubhouses and cafés opened across the country, welcoming workers and offering a space for socialist meetings and societies. Blatchford opened the Clarion Café on Market Street on 31st October 1908. Filled with remarkable murals and artworks from socialist artists William Morris and Walter Crane, the café remained open, serving the workers of central Manchester for over twenty years. Mary began working at the café and would have listened daily to the socialist meetings and discussions happening across the tables that she waited on. It was most likely through one of these meetings that Mary came across the speaker that would encourage her to use her voice and practice exactly what the customers of the Clarion preached – strength in unity and the power of the trade unions. As we have seen before, a spark is often needed, or a moment of inspiration. For Ellen Wilkinson, it was Katherine Glaiser, for Lydia Becker it was Barbara Bodichon, and for Mary Quaile, it was Margaret Bondfield.

Margaret Bondfield had long been a champion for women workers; she fought for better rights for female shopkeepers and helped establish the National Federation of Women Workers. An ardent supporter of the Labour movement, Margaret became the organising secretary of the Women's Labour League in 1908. She travelled the country delivering a series of talks for the league and like many other women trade unionists, became a household name. It's unsurprising, given Margaret's reputation and Mary's interest in the Labour movement and trade unionism, that Mary went to see her speak.

Whilst working at the Clarion café, Mary helped form the Café Workers Union, becoming secretary in 1910. The 1911 census records Mary as living at home with her parents and her six siblings at their house in Pimlott Street.

Mary's job is recorded as: *Clerk - Women's Union*. Although it doesn't give much detail, Mary had left the Café Workers Union, and joined the Manchester and Salford and District Trades Council as secretary. Mary worked to secure proper and fair employment for working women, working across different sectors, unions and trades. During the First World War, women began to take over the roles of men and more women needed representation by trade unions. Although many unions supported the war and suspended strikes, Mary continued to fight for women workers at home.

Mary was a pacifist, like many other women on the left, and whilst she strove to support women workers during the First World War, she supported Conscientious Objectors and was a member of the anti-conscription fellowship. After the war ended in 1918, Mary became the women's organiser for the Dock, Wharf and Riverside Workers' Union, which in 1922, merged with the Transport and General Workers Union. The twenties saw a decade of massive social change after the war. Some women were now able to vote and stand as Members of Parliament and yet many women were losing their jobs, as the men who they had replaced returned from war. In 1924, Margaret Bondfield became the first female cabinet minister in the first Labour Government. Mary took her place on the General Council of the TUC and carried on advocating for women workers.

Like many other left-wing activists of the day, Mary was intrigued and inspired by the Russian revolution of 1917. In the spring of 1925, she led a delegation of female trade unionists on a visit across the Soviet Union, visiting a host of factories and schools, amongst other sites. They travelled across the country, and Mary documented the entire trip, writing:

'…a tremendous welcome awaited us with bands, banners, flowers and speeches. One was glad and proud to be a member of the class that demonstrated so plainly their love for the women workers of Britain.'

Mary conducted a thorough report of the visit and overall was impressed by the standards that women workers were treated. She summarised her report in support of the Soviet Union, writing:

'…there is much in Soviet Russia that our workers might do well to study; that so far this experiment has resulted in bringing about enormous benefits for the toiling masses of Russia; that these benefits are lasting and likely to become more widespread…'

Women workers presented the delegation with a banner bearing the inscription: *'To English women delegates of the General council of Trade Unions, Long Live the unity of the Trade Union Movement.'*

Mary left the General Council in 1926 but continued to be involved with the TUC and carried on travelling internationally as a representative of the trade union movement. She remained active in Manchester, becoming Justice of the Peace in 1934. She joined the Manchester Trades Council in 1936 and acted as Treasurer until her death in 1958. Her long service to the trade union movement earned her the TUC silver badge in 1951, one of the first women to receive such an honour.

Mary's story hasn't remained hidden and her story is now shared by the Working Class Movement Library in Salford. Her story does not move around the colours green, white and purple. The fight for equality and the fight for the vote were not the same thing and Mary tells us there was more than one voice speaking at the same time – voices for the vote, voices for freedom, and voices like Mary's, shouting for solidarity, shouting for unity and shouting for women workers.

ESTHER ROPER

The story of a young working-class woman, recently orphaned, fighting against all odds to win her degree and a coveted place in academic society is a success story that would still resonate in newspapers and online today. It seems almost impossible that this could happen to anybody in the 19th century, but it did: to Esther Roper, who was, amongst other things, one of the first women to attend Owen's College and an ardent suffragist. Esther's life story is one of courage, of ambition, and of dedication to the cause of forwarding women's rights.

Esther Gertrude Roper was born on 4th August 1868 to Reverend Thomas Roper, a factory worker turned church minister, and his wife, Annie Craig. Annie Craig had played a huge part in the long spells of missionary work led by Thomas in West Africa. She helped him set up schoolrooms, where she took up the role of school teacher. Esther was their first child and though her mother would have a string of pregnancies, only one more daughter and a son would live past infancy. Thomas Roper, having dedicated most of his life to missionary work accompanied by Annie, died young at the age of thirty-nine. Esther's early life, therefore, was unsettled, as she was so often cared for instead by her grandparents.

When the family returned to Manchester, they struggled to make ends meet, living off the small pension provided by the Church Missionary Society (CMS) after Thomas' death. Although most young women were sent out to work in the textile factories of the city and outer towns to bring in extra income for the household, Esther instead was sent to school. Her mother believed in education for young women and Esther's studies were partly sponsored by the CMS. Esther's father was already an example of how a vocation and studying could change a person's fortunes – his daughter would continue his legacy, when she secured a place at Owen's College, Manchester.

Owen's College was named after Robert Owen, a textile merchant and a social reformer, who had left a bequest on his death for a new college to be built. The college was supported by local social philanthropists, including William Gaskell, Elizabeth Gaskell's husband. The college allowed for the sons of the rising middle classes, of textile merchants and industrialists to attend university, removing the class barrier that often stood in place. In 1886, Esther was accepted into the college as one of the first women ever allowed to study there, as part of a five-year programme that tested the mental and physical health of female students. Esther studied hard and enjoyed university life, choosing to undertake a degree in History. During her time at Owen's College, Esther joined several societies and even edited her first newsletter. When she was in her final year, Esther's mother died and once again she was uprooted from her home, this time responsible for her younger siblings. Esther graduated from Owen's College in 1891, but remained involved with the university for several years with special interest in the well-being and progress of her fellow female students. She remained the president of the Women's Students Debating Society, where she would first meet Christabel Pankhurst.

Esther's interest in women's suffrage had developed at university and she was employed in the coveted position of secretary of the Manchester National Society for Women's Suffrage

(MNSWS). The society had been directionless since the death of Lydia Becker and it's no wonder that Esther, who was young, intelligent and bursting with energy, revived the MNSWS. Esther came from a background of factory workers and was determined that those women were represented and supported too. Whilst many suffragists were concerned with winning the vote on the same terms as men (with a property qualification), Esther was committed to universal suffrage. The committee merged with the national movement, and became a branch of the National Union of Women's Suffrage Societies (NUWSS).

In 1896, Esther would meet the woman who would change her life, define her, and work tirelessly with her to ensure a fair voice for all. Overworked and exhausted, Esther left Manchester to recover in Italy, and whilst there, first laid eyes on Eva Gore-Booth. Eva, the daughter of an Irish aristocrat and landowner, was the sister of Constance Markievicz, who would become infamous for her part in the fight for Irish Home Rule and the Easter Rising of 1916. Eva and Esther's upbringings were worlds away from each other. Eva had been raised in Lissadell House, a grand country house in Country Sligo, where she was educated in French, Latin, and embroidery. Eva was a talented and published poet, and later immortalised her meeting with Esther in verse:

'You whose Love's melody
makes glad the gloom
Of a long labour and a patient
strife
Is not that music greater
than our Life?
Shall not a little song
outlast that doom?'

There have been theories about the nature of Eva and Esther's relationship over the years, but there seems little doubt now that it was a romantic one. Almost immediately after their meeting, Eva left Ireland and moved into Esther's home in Manchester. They lived together until Eva's death in 1926 and were rarely parted. As Esther wrote:

'We spent the days walking and talking on the hillside by the sea. Each was attracted to the work and thoughts of the other, and we soon became friends and companions for life.'

With Eva also committed to the cause for working women and suffrage, together the two women were a formidable force to be reckoned with. In 1903, the couple set up the Lancashire and Cheshire Women's Textile and Other Worker's Committee. Women textile workers made up a vast amount of the workforce across the north west, although many of them were not represented by the trade unions and received less pay and benefits from their employers. They carried out action by peaceful lobbying and one of their first major acts in 1903 helped select the first women's candidate for the General Election. Thorley Smith stood for Wigan and came in second; Eva and Esther campaigned for him across the constituency.

This was the first time anybody had stood as a candidate for women's suffrage. In a statement published in the Manchester Guardian, the committee stated:

'Anyone who wishes to better the position of her fellow-workers and of the thousands of women outside the ranks of skilled cotton operatives who are being overworked and underpaid, should remember that political enfranchisement must precede industrial emancipation…the political disabilities of women have done incalculable harm by cheapening their labour and lowering their position in the industrial world.'

The committee was intertwined with women's enfranchisement, and although Esther remained the secretary of the Manchester National Society for Women's Suffrage, she was an early supporter of the Women's Social and Political Union. The two women had a close friendship with Christabel Pankhurst and supported the early ideals of the WSPU. However, the lack of support for total enfranchisement and Emmeline and Christabel's insistence that they campaigned for the vote only on the same terms as men, led to Eva and Esther distancing themselves from the Pankhursts. After the militant activities began to escalate after 1905, Eva and Esther publicly showed disapproval for these actions, and despite their once close relationship, Christabel broke off all contact with them.

Esther continued to fight for women workers through the committee. She joined Eva when she founded the Barmaids' Political Defence League in 1908. The Liberal government, promising to increase restrictions on public houses, proposed to ban women from working in these establishments, deeming them to be responsible for luring men inside and to the drink. Through a vigorous campaign at the Manchester elections, Eva, Esther and Eva's sister Constance, managed to force out the Liberal MP, Winston Churchill. It was a success for working women everywhere.

Esther continued her long-time interest of journalism from her university days and edited many journals over her lifetime, including *Women's Labour News*, and *Urania*. *Urania* ran between 1916 and 1940 and can be considered the first LGBT+ journal of its time. It challenged and usurped common ideas of gender and sex, promoting fluidity and free love.

Esther lived for another twelve years after Eva's death, without the woman who had been constantly by her side. She used the remainder of her life to publish Eva's poems and literary works, alongside editing and publishing the letters of Constance Markievicz. She lived to see the enfranchisement of all women aged 21 and over in 1928, the very thing that she and Eva had dedicated their entire lives to. In 1938, Esther passed away peacefully at the home she had shared with Eva. She was buried by her side, their joint grave engraved with a quote from the classical poet, Sappho: *'Life that is love is God.'*

ELLEN WILKINSON

'Ellen Wilkinson, I am told, has red hair. But this, my chivalry takes for granted, is not her fault. Neither is it her fault that she was educated in Manchester. Manchester can happen to anybody.'

Manchester can happen to anyone – but Manchester is lucky that 'Red Ellen' was born and raised in the city. Radical, forthright and resolute, Ellen Wilkinson was one of the first women to be voted into parliament, six years after women were enfranchised. From her earliest days at Westminster, Ellen challenged dusty and outdated traditions, took on every kind of misogynistic behaviour, and actively advocated against austerity, poverty and war.

Although she is famous for leading the Jarrow March, Ellen's time in and out of parliament was filled with many more deeds of bravery and fights for justice. Her success, it may seem, was almost impossible. How did a short, working-class woman from Manchester rise to become Member of Parliament for Middlesbrough, and the only woman to be voted into the Labour Party? The answer is hard graft, a bright energy and a gift of oration matched with the best political speakers of the day. Ellen suffered extreme misogyny in the press and fought against the many prejudices in place against her. Ultimately, she defied everybody who doubted her and rose to become one of the most prominent, out-spoken and charismatic politicians of the early 20th century.

Ellen was born on 8th October 1891 in Chorlton-Upon-Medlock, to Richard Wilkinson, an insurance agent and Ellen Wood of 41 Coral Street. It was a traditional working-class household and Ellen was raised as a strict Methodist alongside her siblings, Annie, Richard and Harold. She was entirely unromantic about her childhood and upbringing, acknowledging the struggles of her parents feeding four mouths. Whilst in many working-class households, women would also work to bring in extra income, Ellen's mother had suffered so much in childbirth that she was too ill to work. Annie, Ellen's elder sister, would have been made to find employment as soon as she could leave school.

This was a time before the National Health Service (NHS), and so when Ellen also fell ill at a young age, she missed years of school. Despite this, Ellen was bright and excelled upon her return, and attended the Ardwick Higher Elementary School. Even at an early age, Ellen recognised the issues and imbalances within the education system; from the dated methods of teaching to the 'sausage factory' manner in which school children were driven through school. Ellen was lucky; she had won a place at the Elementary school through a scholarship and later became painfully aware of the lack of opportunity for young working-class people to advance through the school system as it stood. These early inklings were a sign of the change that she would one day stir up on the benches of the House of Commons.

It seems unimaginable that somebody as passionate about politics as Ellen would not have been exposed to radical thinking at an early age, but the Wilkinson household was not a particularly political place. Her father, though a trade unionist, did not align with the Independent Labour Party, believing that social reform was born from personal hard work and pulling one's self 'out of the gutter'. Indeed, Ellen too might have never have engaged with socialism but for a mock debate at school, at which she was asked to stand in for the role of the socialist candidate. Ellen's research for the task led her to radical thinkers such as Samuel Blatchford and her interest was captured.

Alongside her father, she would attend meetings at the Free Trade Hall and their local Methodist church for free lectures on subjects such as philosophy, sociology, ethics and politics. What little interest she had in the education she received at school was piqued here, and she began to read more at home, around these subjects that fascinated her. Ellen remained an avid reader all her life, eventually publishing her own books, both on the political affairs of her constituents and the nation at large, as well as a semi-autobiographical novel, *Clash*.

Careers for young women at the time were limited; her sister was a dressmaker (although on the 1911 census she was listed as a dressmaker/school teacher), but Ellen's parents recognised Ellen's brightness, and rather than sending her into employment to raise the family finances, she was sent into higher education. Ellen was first sent to train as a teacher, spending time studying both in and outside of classrooms, which she hated. With a thirst for learning and an early interest in politics, Ellen won a scholarship to the University of Manchester in 1910, where she studied for a degree in history.

Here, Ellen's political activism flourished. She had been captivated at a young socialist meeting by Katherine Bruce Glasier, a prominent trade unionist and early advocate of woman's suffrage, and subsequently immersed herself into the left-wing political scene. Whilst at university, Ellen joined the University Fabian Society and became a committed member of the Women's Union and the Women's Students Debating Society. She was even engaged, briefly, to a fellow would-be radical, but broke it off, preferring to concentrate on the bright future that lay ahead of her.

After graduating with a 2:1, Ellen's first role was as a local organiser for the Manchester Society of Women's Suffrage, under the mentorship of leader Margaret Ashton. Ellen's presence at outdoor meetings was incredibly powerful. Despite her youth, Ellen's appearance – her diminutive height, her blazing red hair and her bold stature – gave her a dynamism and charisma that drew in crowds. She was a remarkably gifted orator, even when facing jeers and taunts from the crowd – she was notably called 'carrots' and had vegetables thrown at her.

During The First World War, Ellen's dedication to working women flourished. Whilst volunteering for the Women's Labour League in 1915, she became an organiser for the Amalgamated Union of Co-operative Employees (AUCE). Often working alongside fellow trade unionist Mary Quaile, Ellen strove for better pay and conditions for working women in industries across the country. During this time the close friendships she forged in Manchester remained a crucial part of her life and she continued to work alongside Margaret Ashton and Annot Robinson. Her job involved an immense amount of travel, working all hours of the day. Ellen began to display the tireless work ethic that she would later become renowned for in parliament.

At the heart of her work was her commitment to socialism. Ellen joined the Communist Party in 1920 and attended the Conference of Communist Women in Moscow in 1921. Her membership in the Communist Party was not made to last, although she kept the beliefs and principles close to her heart for the rest of her life. As her political star began to rise, Ellen had to choose between putting her faith into the Labour party or the Communist Party of Great Britain.

In 1924, Ellen was finally elected to parliament, winning the Middlesbrough seat and becoming the only woman of the opposition. Ellen's victory in Middlesbrough, from afar, seemed unlikely. She was a young, unmarried woman, whilst the voters in her constituency was mainly made up of industrial men, but they opened their arms to the woman who would fight for them furiously. Her maiden speech spoke out for the many women still disenfranchised by the Representation of the People Act and yet Ellen actively denounced the she would be an MP simply for women. In the House of Commons, her passionate rhetoric and her modern appearance drew attention. She was so small she had to stand on her despatch box to get to her seat and she immediately came under scrutiny for her bright dresses and loud fashions. Nancy Astor, the Conservative MP for Plymouth, famously dressed in black, masculine suits, and privately advised Ellen to dress more suitably, but she didn't heed her advice, eventually stating in an interview: *'Can't a woman do her work just as well in a dress of bright colours?'*

Ellen was a modern woman during a time of huge political and social liberation for women. She never married, choosing instead to put her career first, although she had long-standing affairs with political cartoonist Frank Horrabin and deputy Labour leader Herbert Morrison.

Parliament was not equipped for women. They were separated from the male MPS and placed in an office. The space where they were expected to work Ellen dourly named 'the tomb', lamenting there was just one coat hook for all the female MPs and no specified bathroom.

Ellen was voted out of parliament in 1931, when the Conservative party won a landslide victory. Although devoid of the vocation that she had given so much to, Ellen didn't stop campaigning against poverty, fascism and social injustice. In her time out of the House, Ellen's international journalism began to gain merit as she wrote about the treatment of communists and political prisoners in Nazi Germany.

Ellen returned to the House in 1935, for perhaps her most famous achievement yet. Economic depression had hit the north of England hard. In Jarrow, the shipyards, their biggest form of employment and profit began to close and the town was left in poverty. In October 1936, Ellen marched with over two hundred men from the town, mostly war veterans, to present a petition to parliament. The Jarrow Crusade became infamous; it brought attention to the plight of not only Jarrow, but to all the industrial towns that had been crippled by the state of the country. Ellen left the march briefly to attend the Labour Party Conference. She demanded action, rejecting claims that there should be another report filed about the town, stating:

'Is there not one pore of the working man's body that has not been card-indexed?'

The petition was rejected, but the Jarrow Crusade had a long-lasting legacy, exposing the people of Britain to the harsh realities of austerity and the recession, dictating the need for a post-war welfare state. Ellen later wrote The Town That Was Murdered, an account of the march and the impact of the recession on industrial towns in Jarrow.

During the second World War, Ellen, ever committed to fighting fascism, worked as a junior minister in the coalition government and as parliamentary secretary to Herbert Morrison. Ellen's work during the war was focused primarily on the shelter welfare and policy, and established the women's guard of fire-watchers – women who could watch for the blitz fires and prevent them from spreading. Ellen rallied women to support the war effort, stating that 'women power' was needed.

In 1945, a Labour Government was voted into parliament, winning by a landslide. Although Ellen hadn't always seen eye to eye with Clement Attlee, the new Prime Minister, she was made a part of his cabinet, taking on the role of Minister for

Education. Ellen's tenacity and determination shone in the post-war cabinet. She successfully implemented the 1941 Education Act, ensuring the school leaving age was risen and free milk was given in schools. Ellen had achieved her success partially because of the education, and access to education, that she had received and so was determined to give that back, supporting university scholarships across the country, particularly for the young men and women who had fought in the war.

Ellen's ill health could have easily dominated and dictated her life, as it had done when she was a child. However, she never let it stop her or slow her down, even during the arduous hours of the Jarrow Crusade. Ellen died of an accidental overdose on 6th February 1947, when she contracted bronchitis, at the age of 54. She died in office, furiously carrying on the work she was incredibly committed to. Ellen's name now lends itself to a school for girls in London and a building at the University of Manchester, but her legacy is more than her impact on education.

Ellen Wilkinson was a modern woman and championed the future of women, in politics and beyond. With enough tenacity, enough determination and enough courage, Ellen proved that a young woman could achieve anything.

And still can.

Manchester suffragette banner, 1908 © People's History Museum

'I incite this meeting to rebellion'

Walk through Stevenson Square in the Northern Quarter of Manchester today and one is met with bars and cafés in keeping with the fashionable part of the city it has become. It is difficult to imagine what it might have looked like in 1908 – still busy with shops and on the cusp of the working-class districts of Ancoats, different crowds would have frequented the square. A short walk from the first female statue in Manchester (Queen Victoria), Stevenson Square in the early 1900s was a place for political reform meetings and open-air discussions. It was here, after the arrest of Christabel Pankhurst and Annie Kenney in October 1905, that the suffragettes gathered to protest this unjust treatment, and on 21nd June 1908 a banner was unfurled in the square. These two incidents, almost three years apart, demonstrate the speed at which the militant movement grew and the rise of Emmeline Pankhurst as the leader of the fight for the vote.

The unveiling of the banner was an event unto itself, carried out in preparation for the following day, when tens of thousands of people would gather in Hyde Park for the biggest women's suffrage rally the country had ever seen. The Manchester branch of the Women's Social and Political Union (WSPU) had commissioned the banner for the occasion and it was crafted by the staff at Thomas Brown & Co. from a deep, purple velvet, bordered by embroidered green letters that spell out: *Manchester Women's Social & Political Union*. In large gold letters set against the vivid purple backdrop, the banner reads:

First in the Fight
Founded By Mrs Pankhurst
1903

A piper marched the banner into the square in a wagonette with Mary Gawthorpe and Rona Robinson. Mary had been an organiser for the WSPU in Leeds, having joined after the arrests of Christabel and Annie, and Rona Robinson, her fellow WSPU organiser, was the first woman in the country to achieve a first-class degree in Chemistry (from Owen's College, Manchester). Like fellow Manchester academics Esther Roper and Marie Stopes, Rona's sex meant she was unable to graduate, but still she utilised her degree and became a dye researcher, until the WSPU took her away from her work full-time. Lancashire MP, Victor Grayson, gave a speech at the unveiling, as did a Miss Williamson (possibly Lillian, one of the women involved in the attack on Manchester Art Gallery), and Sam Brooks, secretary for the Men's League of Women's Suffrage. It was the calm before the storm, with all the excitement and anticipation of a child's Christmas Eve, building up for the next day, when women from across the country would come together and raise their voices as one to demand the vote.

The Headquarters of the WSPU had left Manchester by this time. It was inevitable that one of the fastest-growing political organisations would need to be in the capital, on the doorstep of Parliament. But the Manchester branch still bore a fierce pride that their city had been the belly in which the fire of the campaign had brewed; it is no wonder they wanted the rest of the country to share in their pride.

The moment of the banner's unveiling can be pinpointed, perhaps, as the moment that the early radical suffragists began to fade out of public memory and history. What **Lydia Becker**, one of the early leaders of the constitutional Manchester National Society of Women's Suffrage, would have thought of the actions of the WSPU can be guessed. Perhaps her thoughts would have been similar to Margaret Ashton's, who in 1905 had written a letter to the Manchester Guardian, distancing the Women's Liberal Association from the WSPU and expressing the strong opinion that the actions of Annie and Christabel, and any resulting militant action, would delay women being granted the vote for years. The North of England Society for Women's Suffrage, which was part of the National Union of Women's Suffrage Societies (NUWSS), also condemned their actions.

There is always a clash between generations – the older thinking they know best and the younger feeling it is time for fresh, new ideas. This clash can be seen in Manchester, as the sun rose on the militant movement and set just a little on the suffragists. The NUWSS remained the largest organisation in the country, their actions similarly heralded and vilified, but still, the WSPU commanded the headlines with their increasingly daring and unlawful actions.

Many suffragettes and suffragists make up the long-list for the statue campaign, but there are many who were the foot-soldiers of the movement, those who were force-fed, beaten, arrested, assaulted and abused, who are left off the list. There are three Pankhursts on the list. Although it is important to recognise the leaders of the campaign, there will always be anonymous and nameless women who gave their all to the fight for the vote and will never be remembered or known as such.

One of the missing suffragists was one of the oldest and most revered of the campaigners and had given her full support to the militant campaign. Elizabeth Wolstenholme-Elmy, the first secretary of the Manchester Society for Women's Suffrage in 1867, became an early supporter. She herself is a gaping absence from the long-list. Small and frail in appearance, Elizabeth had been involved in some of the most challenging and ferocious campaigns for women's equality and enfranchisement, from the early campaigns for the vote to the advancement of female education. She had come from a strict religious family in Cheetham Hill, who had been horrified when she had fallen pregnant and refused to marry her partner, fellow radical Benjamin Elmy. To please their families, Elizabeth had married. This early tenacity and refusal to conform to social norms was a sign of what was to come. When the suffragettes marched to Hyde Park in 1908, Elizabeth was given a prestigious place next to Emmeline in the procession.

Sylvia Pankhurst claimed that many of the women in the room on 10th October 1903 were linked to working-class causes, but traditionally, those who had the social and financial freedoms to lead the campaigns were middle-class women. The leaders all identified mill and factory towns as fertile recruiting grounds for gaining women's support, but few working-class women could give up their working lives to become disciples of the movement. Some, however, did just that. Whilst the three Pankhurst sisters were indeed the most infamous siblings in the WSPU, the Kenney sisters gave just as much loyalty, hard work, and sacrifice to the movement. Annie and Jessie were both organisers across the country and were two of the only working-class women in the inner circle of the WSPU.

Annie was instrumental in the recruitment of working-class women. On the first deputation to parliament, Annie wore the traditional shawl and clogs of a mill girl, emphasising her role as a representative of working women. The Pankhursts had diligently trained her as a public speaker, and those who saw her noted her powerful oration and the passion in her words. By 1914, Annie was running the WSPU under the instruction of Christabel, who remained in Paris; Annie travelled there almost every weekend to see her. It was the fight for the vote that took Annie away from a life of mill work, across seas and across continents. Although she followed the Pankhursts into the Women's Party, formed from the WSPU on the enfranchisement of women, she retired from politics after the 1918 election. Unlike many other women's suffrage campaigners, Annie now has a statue in her hometown of Oldham, representing the many working-class women who, like her, fought for the vote.

During the formative years of the militant campaign, the women of Manchester risked gaol time and public abuse during their work for the WSPU, often with little or no immediate reward, such as Annot Robinson, a Scottish teacher who had moved to Manchester in 1907. Having previously been involved with the Dundee branch of the WSPU, Annot had divided loyalties between the WSPU and socialism, being an active member of the Independent Labour Party (ILP) and an organiser for the Women's Labour League. Annot was imprisoned at Holloway Gaol in February 1908 following her involvement in a suffragette raid on the House of Commons, and was arrested again in July 1908, when addressing a crowd of hundreds in Albert Square. Like many other women, particularly those still committed to the Labour party, Annot grew disillusioned with the Pankhurst

leadership and joined the NUWSS. On the outbreak of the First World War she became one of the first members, alongside Margaret Ashton and Ellen Wilkinson, of the Women's International League for Peace and Freedom. Annot's name is little known in Manchester, although her name now features on the plinth of the Millicent Garrett Fawcett statue in London, alongside fifty-five other suffrage campaigners, including Elizabeth-Wolstenholme-Elmy, Ellen Wilkinson, Eva Gore-Booth, Margaret Ashton, and Teresa Billington-Greig.

One glaring omission is Hannah Mitchell, whose autobiography, *Hard Way Up*, was instrumental to early historians studying the lives of working-class suffragettes. Hannah came to suffrage through socialism, from the rolling hills of Derbyshire. She joined the WSPU almost at once and, like Annie Kenney, was a force to be reckoned with as she recruited working women from across Lancashire to the cause. Although her husband, Gibbon, was a socialist and a supporter of women's suffrage, Hannah shed light on the deep-rooted gender roles that were still prevalent within these marriages, as despite her work and her campaigning, she was still expected to have dinner on the table and keep the house spotless. As the Pankhursts turned away from working women, however, and ran the WSPU with a much more autocratic rule, Hannah became disillusioned and joined the Women's Freedom League (WFL). There are no Women's Freedom League representatives on the statue long-list. In fact, aside from Margaret Ashton and Ellen Wilkinson, the wider breadth of the organisations who fought for the vote are barely represented. The green, white and purple of the WSPU prevails here, as it does in public memory and heritage.

And yet, the story of the 'First in the Fight' banner, held aloft that day in Stevenson Square, is a testament to the foot-soldiers of the campaign. It was marched through Alexandra Park to celebrate the release of imprisoned suffragettes, it stood alongside Emmeline in Heaton Park, and of course, on the Manchester platform on Women's Sunday in 1908. In 1939, the banner was hoisted high once more to celebrate twenty-one years of enfranchisement for women. By 1951, the banner, along with suffragette ephemera, was lost.

The banner, in fact, was in the safe-keeping of working-class suffragette and embroiderer Elizabeth Ellen Chatterton and remained in the family for over forty years, alongside her WSPU sash and her brooch from Women's Sunday, both of which are now lost. An extraordinary turn of events led to the banner being discovered in the offices of a charity shop in 2017, and after a successful Crowdfunder, was accessioned by the People's History Museum. Due to the diligent family research undertaken by Elizabeth's great-granddaughter, the full history of the banner was revealed.

Although it is emblazoned with Emmeline's name, the banner was made by working-class women, for working-class women to march under. For all the nameless women in the city of Manchester who gave everything to the fight for enfranchisement, this banner and the symbolic colours of purple for dignity, white for purity, and green for hope represent their struggle, their reasons for fighting, just as much as it represents Emmeline. The statue too represents more than Emmeline. It represents every woman who handed out a copy of *The Suffragette*, or boycotted the census; every suffragist and suffragette who marched, sang, signed petitions or smashed windows for the cause. Their names may not be listed, their faces may not be carved in bronze, but their legacy lives on through the continued radical actions of Manchester women.

LYDIA BECKER

A vast number of names, faces, people and places have been remembered in history, and in memory. Many of the women here, such as Emmeline Pankhurst, are still household names, celebrated for their great deeds, actions and the change they brought about. Some however, are lost; in the case of Lydia Becker, once a household name and immediately recognised in any cartoon or cruel depiction the newspapers printed of her, her story has been overshadowed by later, more radical activists. But this early campaigner for women's suffrage was once at the heart of the movement and made a lasting impact on the campaign and its efforts, until her death in 1890.

Lydia Ernestine Becker was born on 27th February 1827, in Cooper Street, Manchester, to a British mother and German father. Hannibal Becker, Lydia's father, ran a chemical works, giving the family a middle-class income and upbringing. A blue plaque marks the family's home at Foxdenton Hall, Middleton. One of fifteen children, Lydia was educated at home and after the death of her mother, remained at home to help raise her siblings. Lydia took on the typical domestic role in the household as the eldest daughter and remained unmarried. Despite this, she managed to spend time abroad, travelling to her father's home in Thuringia, Germany.

Lydia sympathised with working-class women and their lack of access to education and opportunity, but she remained politically disengaged. The city of Manchester had seen struggle for reform and social change for years; Lydia had grown up in the aftermath of the Peterloo massacre and Chartism and was unable to avoid the poverty and marked difference in living conditions between the rich and the poor.

In her book, *The Suffragette Movement - An Intimate Account Of Persons And Ideals*, Sylvia Pankhurst described Lydia Becker as 'an old maid' when she stepped into the world of politics. True, Lydia was thirty-nine years old when she became the secretary of the Manchester Committee for Women's Suffrage, but this isn't entirely fair. She may have lived her life quietly, but it was well seasoned, exploring her interests and setting up spaces for them to be shared and brought into public life. Her scientific interests and her published works on astronomy and botany achieved her accolades in the science community. She wrote a manual *An Introduction to Botany*, and won a Gold Medal from the Horticultural Society. These achievements led her into correspondence with the father of evolution, Charles Darwin. She would send him samples of her work studying local flora, especially primroses. Despite her comfortable position in life, Lydia was faced with the same barriers and frustrations as other middle-class women, unable to progress or advance in society and often defined by a husband and family life.

This love of science led her to start the Manchester Ladies Literary Society, for women like her to gather and discuss their scientific interests. Many identical organisations in the city banned women from joining. Lydia showed her determination and early commitment to gender equality when she set up the society. Perhaps her greatest coup for the first meeting of this small women's society, was securing a paper from Charles Darwin, sent after a personal request from Lydia, to be read at the inaugural gathering in January 1867.

Illustration by **Maisy Summer**

It was Lydia's constant investment in knowledge and interest in the wider scientific community that, in 1866, led her to a lecture by Barbara Bodichon, a suffrage campaigner, at a meeting of the Social Sciences Association, entitled the *Enfranchisement of Women*. Lydia was enthused and, to an extent, radicalised by the lecture, setting her on a course towards the campaign that would dominate the rest of her life.

At this stage, the campaign for women's suffrage was not a new idea. Petitions had been presented to parliament as early as 1834 and Manchester, unsurprisingly, already had a small committee led by Elizabeth Wolstenholme-Elmy, that collected petitions and spoke widely across the city and the surrounding towns on the matter.

Unlike many of the other committee members, Lydia had no previous connections to political campaigns in the city and had no personal links or comrades who could have informed her of the already energised activity for the enfranchisement of women. However, Lydia had been inspired by what she had heard at the lecture and penned her own article on the subject. *The Contemporary Review* at the time was looking for articles on the matter of enfranchisement and with the support of fellow suffragist Emily Davies, Lydia's article was published. The article brought her into the periphery of the already active suffragists in Manchester. Elizabeth Wolstenholme-Elmy, who, recognising a potentially fierce ally, called upon Lydia and invited her to join the committee. Quickly, Elizabeth Wolstenholme-Elmy handed over the role of honourable secretary to Lydia, later stating:

'I was only glad to transfer my work in this post into her all too capable hands.'

Lydia took up the role with gusto and soon became acquainted with other social reformers in the city, most notably Dr Richard Pankhurst, and Ursula and Jacob Bright. Lydia struck Manchester hard, immediately printing over ten thousand pamphlets containing her article to be spread across the city. She formalised the committee and began to strengthen its national connections to similar organisations in London, joining up their petitions and creating a smoother approach to cross-committee campaigning.

As the committee was still reliant on Members of Parliament to champion their cause in the House of Commons, the Manchester Society for Women's Suffrage, as it became in 1867, worked with Liberal MPs John Stuart Mill and Jacob Bright to have their case heard. That year, Stuart Mill had presented a bill in Parliament that would have amended the Reform Act to allow women to have the vote on the same terms as men (there were still substantial limitations to male suffrage also). It was defeated by 194 votes to 73. Although parliament were still not paying attention, Lydia was leading activity that was making the rest of the country take notice.

Sylvia Pankhurst described Lydia in her book, as:

'A woman of plain and solid exterior, her heavy features appealed to the popular mind as typical of the 'strong-minded' woman…possessing no remarkable gifts of intellect or oratory, she was apt in making a clear, concise statement of her case.'

It is perhaps a little unfair. Lydia travelled across the country delivering lectures and talks on the subject of enfranchisement and was an endearing and impressive speaker. It was, as Sylvia also noted, her qualities as an organiser and her ability to utilise the people around her, that made her so successful – a trait seen early on, in her correspondence with Charles Darwin. Soon, Lydia's image became known across the country, as her constant lobbying gained more attention. Political cartoons emerged, particularly of her and Liberal MP Jacob Bright, deriding her as a spinster and him as weak-willed. This did not deter Lydia, or Jacob; they continued to lobby for the vote in Manchester and across the country.

Perhaps the most famous act that Lydia conducted whilst secretary of the society was concerned with the case of Lily Maxwell. In the lead up to the 1867 by-election in Manchester, it was discovered that Lily Maxwell, an elderly shopkeeper based in Chorlton-Upon-Medlock, had been listed on the voting register by mistake. Error or not, Lily had the right to vote and on election day was escorted to Chorlton Town Hall and cast her vote for Jacob Bright. It was an incredible coup for the suffragists, as over a thousand female property owners were spurred on to register to vote, although only a small number succeeded in doing so. This was the first act outside of petitions and collecting signatures that Lydia had orchestrated. It demonstrated an inkling of future action the militant suffragettes would undertake, of rallying against the powers in charge and undermining political laws as best they could.

In 1869, the Municipal Franchise Act was passed, granting some women the vote in local elections and the opportunity to become Poor Law Guardians. But this was not the end for Lydia and the society. They began to publish the *Women's Suffrage Journal*, which Lydia edited for twenty years. Lydia came up against other members of the Society when, in 1870, the Conservatives came into power. The MP that would have taken the Suffrage Bill forward, that Jacob Bright and John Stuart Mill had been pushing for in the House of Commons, wished to add a clause which would prohibit married women from voting. Lydia, although resistant, grudgingly accepted this, believing that part suffrage would lead the way to all women getting the vote.

Lydia's campaigning was not restricted to suffrage and she worked across other societies to secure equality for women. Not only was she treasurer of the Married Women's Property Committee, protecting a woman's property from her husband,

she was then elected to the Manchester School Board, where she fought for equal education. She argued that boys should learn domestic skills as well as women, to avoid wives being treated as, in her words, 'domestic slaves.' She was heavily involved in the repeal of the Contagious Diseases Act, which allowed the police to arrest and search women suspected of prostitution, to prevent the spread of venereal diseases. Men were not party to this law and didn't have to be stopped or searched. It was deeply misogynistic and many social reformers were outraged. After being barred from the male group, the Ladies National Association for the Repeal of the Contagious Diseases Acts was set up in 1869, with Josephine Butler, a fierce feminist and social campaigner, at the helm. Unsurprisingly, Lydia joined the campaign and the act was repealed in 1886.

Towards the end of her life, Lydia had become a household name, synonymous with women's suffrage. She became the secretary of the National Society for Women's Suffrage as the campaign went from strength to strength. Although her ailing health prevented her from travelling and speaking as she had done in previous years, she still made an impression, particularly on the teenage Emmeline Pankhurst, who was taken to one of Lydia's public talks in Manchester in 1874. In 1890, whilst travelling in Switzerland for her health, Lydia contracted diphtheria and died on 18th July, in Geneva.

The taunts and depictions that Lydia Becker faced in political cartoons is something she shares with female politicians and activists today. Time and time again, women in the public eye are sneered at for how they look and not what they think, do, or say. We do not know what Lydia thought about these depictions of herself, with everything about her that didn't fit into the conventional box of beauty, especially her famous, wire-rimmed round glasses. But Lydia represents something about Manchester so powerful and so unique; she embodied the common saying: *'What Lancashire does today, the rest of the world will do tomorrow.'* Her forward thinking and her energy revitalised the campaign for suffrage at a time when it so desperately needed it. The suffragists and suffragettes that followed in her stead owed her a debt of gratitude, as women across the city and indeed across the country, do today.

CHRISTABEL PANKHURST

'How long you women have been trying for the vote. For my part, I need to get it.'

Emmeline Pankhurst recorded in her autobiography that Christabel once 'startled' her with this statement. This single, simple declaration sums up Christabel's approach to the fight for women's suffrage. Her drive, determination and sometime ruthlessness, was both idolized and feared by her fellow campaigners and her adversaries. If Emmeline was the general of the Women's Social and Political Union (WSPU), then her loyal lieutenant, her right-hand woman, was undoubtedly her eldest daughter. Charismatic, beautiful and powerful, Christabel ran the WSPU, alongside her mother, with an iron fist.

There needn't be a lot of sifting through sources, journals, letters, or books to unearth Christabel's history. The legacy of her power across the organisation, her inspiration to the other women and her command of their deeds and words can be found in her autobiography, as well as the memoirs of not only her mother and sisters, but her fellow suffragettes and suffragists.

Her resolve drove the WSPU to victory. Her actions on that fateful day in October 1903 would shape the suffragette movement forever and her subsequent arrest and later, her flight to Paris,

show a daring that she shared with her mother. Whilst her sisters drifted from Emmeline in later life, their relationships fractioning beyond repair, Christabel remained Emmeline's daughter very much until the end.

Christabel Pankhurst was born on 22nd September 1880 in Manchester, the first child of Emmeline Pankhurst, nee Goulden, and Dr Richard Pankhurst. Emmeline and Richard's love and consequent marriage was founded on their shared zeal for political and social activism, something they would impart on each of their children. Christabel was Emmeline and Richard's first child, and she remained Emmeline's favourite until her mother's death in 1928; they formed an incredibly close bond, that overshadowed the relationships Emmeline held with her other daughters.

The Pankhurst family moved to London when Christabel was five years old, taking a house in Russell Square. The house at Russell Square was buzzing with exciting conversation and debate, with the Pankhursts playing host to social reformers and agitators from across the country, including William Morris, Keir Hardie, Annie Besant, Tom Mann and many more. Christabel and her younger sisters were expected by their parents to be part of these meetings and to engage in the conversation. Despite being known in later life as a powerful strategist and confident speaker, this was a skill she built up throughout her childhood, quietly learning from her parents' associates. Richard and Emmeline were early advocates of women's suffrage and helped to form the Women's Franchise League, hosting a conference in

Illustration by **Laura Bohill**

their home that Christabel and Sylvia enthusiastically assisted with. They handed out leaflets and set up a tea room for the delegates. In her autobiography, *My Own Story*, Emmeline wrote of her daughters:

'As they grew older we used to talk about the suffrage, and I was sometimes rather frightened by their youthful confidence in the prospect, which they considered certain, of the success of the movement.'

The sisters demonstrated their fascination and enthusiasm for politics early on. On one occasion, the three Pankhurst sisters decided to give speeches to their parents and extended family. Christabel and Sylvia were under-confident and struggled to deliver; Adela, who was perhaps the strongest public speaker of the three, delivered hers perfectly without notes. Despite the youngest sister's performative personality, Christabel was undoubtedly the leader of the siblings; when she left home to stay with the Blatch family in Basingstoke, Sylvia described life having 'lost its savour.' The Pankhurst siblings were not sent to school until they moved back to Manchester almost a decade later, with Emmeline determined that their individual characters and passions should flourish without the constraint of other children and classrooms. It was Christabel's idea for her and Sylvia to teach each other, rather than the financially strained Pankhursts hiring a governess. The sisters and their parents suffered hardships during their time in London; Christabel's only brother, Frank, died at four years old, and Emerson's, the arts and furnishings shop that Emmeline had opened with a hope to support the family, closed down.

Knowing they could lead a better quality of life in Manchester, the Pankhurst family moved back in 1893, to the leafy, middle class suburb of Victoria Park. Emmeline and Richard joined the Independent Labour Party (ILP). The Pankhurst siblings were sent to the Manchester High School for Girls. Often isolated from the other children due to their parents' socialist and agnostic values, Christabel was frustrated by the regulations and formalities of school and did not try hard in her classes. Unlike Sylvia and Adela, who both had emotional temperaments and were inclined to sulk and feel jealous at Emmeline's affection for their elder sibling, Christabel was more reserved and kept her feelings close to her chest. After leaving school, she continued to take lessons in French, dress-making and logic, before she too became involved with the ILP.

Christabel had her first foray into public politics during the Boggart Hole Clough dispute. In 1896, the council, disturbed by the rise in support for the ILP, banned political meetings at the park. The ILP continued to host their meetings there, as there was no by-law in place to prohibit political meetings, but Keir Hardie and other speakers were arrested. The Pankhursts put themselves at the heart of the public debate, with Emmeline speaking at one of the meetings and narrowly avoiding arrest. Christabel was invited to speak at the ILP conference, encouraged by Hardie and her parents. Despite her growing interest in politics, Christabel was directionless after leaving school and contemplated going into dress-making whilst visiting Europe with her mother.

In 1898, whilst Christabel and Emmeline were in Geneva, a telegram from Sylvia arrived. At the news of Richard Pankhurst's illness, they rushed home, only to be met with the news of his death as they arrived into Manchester by train. The Pankhurst family were emotionally and financially devastated. Christabel returned to Geneva and Emmeline struggled to establish a new income for the family. She re-opened Emerson's, her arts and furnishing shop, at 30 King Street in Manchester and took a job as a registrar. Horrified by the conditions in which women were working, Emmeline credited this role in spurring her demand for women's suffrage further.

The role that Christabel played in bringing the family back towards organised suffrage activity, however, can't be ignored. After her father's death, it was Christabel's early interest in the Manchester National Society for Women's Suffrage that helped reignite Emmeline and Sylvia's interest in the cause.

It must have been a frustrating time for Christabel, who had been travelling in Europe, to come back to the Pankhursts' new, smaller lodgings at 62 Nelson Street and to help look after her younger siblings, particularly Harry and Adela. Working in her mother's shop bored her and she struggled to find a output for her sharp intelligence.

It was whilst attending a meeting of the Women's Students Debating Society that Christabel met Eva Gore-Booth and Esther Roper. Eva and Esther were already well-known campaigners for women's suffrage and better working rights for women workers. Esther was the secretary of the Manchester National Society for Women's Suffrage (MNSWS) and together the couple travelled across the county of Lancashire to champion this cause. Eva Gore-Booth had fallen in love with Esther in Italy whilst they both recuperated from illness and had given up her privileged life as the daughter of an Irish aristocrat to live with Esther in Manchester. Christabel forged a close friendship with Eva, who in a sense took Christabel under her political wing. Christabel was encouraged by Esther and Eva's reenergising of the campaign for women's suffrage and subsequently joined the MNSWS.

Throughout the late 1800s and the early 1900s, Christabel supported and campaigned for the causes that Eva Gore-Booth and Esther Roper had drawn her into, causes that no doubt her father would equally have valued had he been alive. Although in later life Christabel moved away from Richard Pankhurst's political leanings, they still held resonance with her in the first forays into the campaigns for the vote. Christabel was originally impressed with the Independent Labour Party's (ILP) commitment to the question of women's suffrage, and, with Eva and Esther, travelled to speak on the subject to Trade Unions, encouraging them to consider the question. It was at this time that Christabel, with Eva's support, began a law degree at Victoria University in Manchester.

In the ongoing fight for women's suffrage, it became increasingly evident that the lobbying political parties and the use of peaceful methods were not progressing the vote. On the evening of October 13th 1903, Emmeline, Christabel and Sylvia hosted a meeting of women and the decision was made to form a new society, without any party or class specification. This would be a single-issue organisation, dedicated solely to the enfranchisement of women on the same terms as men; with a property qualification and over the age of twenty-one. The Women's Social and Political Union (WSPU) was formed and the motto 'deeds not words' would become the rallying cry of the organisation.

Although Emmeline travelled down to London to lobby at the opening of Parliament, the WSPU failed to capture the attention of the nation until October 1905. As the General Election got closer, Christabel and Annie Kenney attended a meeting at the Free Trade Hall in Manchester, where the Liberal candidate, Edward Grey, was due to speak. Annie Kenney was a young working-class woman from Oldham, who was a loyal member of the WSPU and devoted to Christabel. The two women repeatedly asked the question: 'Will the Liberal Government, if returned, give the vote to women?', holding their small banner reading 'Votes for Women' high. The crowd, mainly men who were outraged at the women's questioning, began to physically attempt to remove them from the hall. As Emmeline described it in her autobiography:

'Hands were lifted to drag her out of her chair, but Christabel threw one arm about her as she stood, and with the other arm warded off the mob, who struck and scratched at her...'

Christabel and Annie were arrested on charges of obstruction and assault. Christabel was accused, perhaps falsely, of spitting in a policeman's face. The women were ordered to either pay a fine or serve a jail sentence. The women chose a jail sentence and the militant campaign for the vote that has become so cemented in our history, was to begin.

After finishing her Law degree with first-class honours in 1906, Christabel took a paid position as chief organiser with the WSPU, and, alongside her mother, became the leader of the organisation. She was the chief strategist, understood the law and was able to offer counsel and support to the suffragettes facing jail sentences. She left the ILP, asserting that the WSPU would not pledge allegiance to any political party. Christabel moved to London and alongside the Pethwick-Lawrences, a wealthy couple who were in the Pankhursts' inner circle, ran the huge operation the WSPU would become. Christabel was an incredibly charismatic and beautiful speaker, not only enrapturing crowds, but the dedication of her fellow suffragettes. They trusted her leadership without question.

As the WSPU grew, dispute and discontent with Emmeline and Christabel's leadership began to break out. Their style was autocratic; their refusal to endorse or campaign for other social issues, as Sylvia Pankhurst did, frustrated many of the suffragettes, and in 1907, prominent members of the WSPU broke away from the Pankhursts to found the Women's Freedom League. Christabel was, to an extent, a ruthless leader and had no qualms about expelling members who did not uphold the WSPU ideals.

In 1911, when the question of suffrage once again failed in parliament, Christabel determined that the militant campaign needed to be stepped up. Plans were put in place to carry out acts of violence and disruption covertly. Christabel was the architect of this plan and hundreds of windows were smashed as thousands of women marched on Westminster. She was almost arrested after the WSPU headquarters were raided in March the following year and had to flee to Paris to escape arrest.

From across the Channel, Christabel still held command over the WSPU, directing from abroad, where she received visits from her mother and Annie Kenney amongst other WSPU members.

When war broke out in 1914, Christabel and Emmeline negotiated with the government to have all WSPU prisoners released on the condition that they would actively support the war effort and put an end to the campaign for the vote. This agreement split the WSPU, many of whom were anti-war or did not want to stop the campaign. As she did with everything, however, Christabel threw herself into this new cause. She organised Women's Right to Serve demonstrations and encouraged the handing out of white feathers to men who had yet to enlist. Ever the tactician, Christabel strategised the war, knowing that women's support here was another path to securing the vote.

After some women were enfranchised in 1918, Christabel formed the Women's Party from the ashes of the WSPU and stood as an MP in Smethwick, but was narrowly defeated by the Labour candidate. After the failure of the Women's Party, Christabel moved to America in 1921. Forever driven by the cause, the former revolutionary and radical Christabel became part of the Second Adventist movement and travelled around the country preaching the second coming of Christ. To the end of her days, Christabel was known for her quintessential British charm and manners. She returned to Britain to care for an ailing Emmeline and was devastated when her mother, the dearest person to her, died in 1928. In their later years, no longer competing for the love and attention of their mother, Christabel and Sylvia somewhat reconciled and wrote to each other until Christabel's death in 1958.

Over the years, Sylvia's memoirs have perhaps clouded people's judgement of Christabel. Fueled by sibling rivalry, Sylvia's picture of Christabel is hardly unbiased and she presented to the world an image of her elder sister as cold, unfeeling, and merciless. And yet, without Christabel, the WSPU and the militant campaign may never have gained the national and international attention it needed to agitate the public and the government. Her vigour and dedication to the militant campaign and her single-mindedness, as she said as a teen to her mother, to win the vote for women, led to her doing just that – no matter what, or who, she had to sacrifice along the way.

SYLVIA PANKHURST

Amidst the many photographs that were taken of the suffragettes, there is one particularly poignant image. A young woman, paintbrush in hand, clearly tracing out the letters 'Votes for Women' on a shop sign, almost nose to nose with the letters. This woman was Sylvia Pankhurst, the daughter of Emmeline and Dr Richard Pankhurst and a founding member of the Women's Social and Political Union (WSPU) in 1903. Her surname holds an incredible legacy, but even without that infamous moniker, the life, deeds and words of Sylvia Pankhurst should be remembered and celebrated as some of the bravest and loudest in the fight for both the vote, and equality, for women everywhere.

Sylvia leant both her artistic and organisational skills to the campaign for women's suffrage. Her political leaning fractured her from her mother and her sister, Christabel, eventually leading to her leaving the WSPU and founding the East End Federation of Women's Suffrage. This bold and lonely action would change the landscape of the movement and cement Sylvia firmly within a radical, left-wing strand of the women's suffrage movement. Although it may seem a departure from the teachings of her mother and sister, who both leaned, eventually, towards the political right, Sylvia's ethics and motives for this were borne from a childhood surrounded by, and determined by, the radical politics of her father and, at one time, her mother.

Sylvia was born on 5th May 1882, to Emmeline and Dr Richard Pankhurst. Although named Estelle, Emmeline's choice, Sylvia was her given middle name chosen by her father and Sylvia would only ever respond to that name. She was the second of what would be five children born to the couple and spent her early years at the family home in Drayton Gardens, Old Trafford. Her childhood mirrored that of her elder sister, Christabel. Richard was a barrister, with close, passionate ties to socialism and later, the Independent Labour Party. When the family left Manchester for London in 1885, their home in Russell Square was brimming with political debate and conversation that Sylvia would have taken an interest in. In her book, *A History of the Women's Suffrage Movement*, Sylvia candidly refers to this when she writes of the formation of the Women's Franchise League (the first meeting of which was held in the Pankhursts' parlour):

'My sister and I, then nine and seven years old, already took a lively interest in the proceedings, and tried as hard as we could to make ourselves useful writing out notices in big, uncertain letters, and distributing leaflets to guests at the three days' conference held in our own home.'

Illustration by **Halah El-Kholy**

47

These serious, almost adult involvements in political campaigning were supported by a loose and free-thinking education; none of the Pankhurst siblings attended school until their return to Manchester in 1893. They went from teaching each other, to being given more informal lessons by their governess at home, who took them on trips to the National Gallery. Both Sylvia and Christabel were shy and more reserved than their younger siblings; Adela was considered the most impressive speaker, a trait she would carry to adulthood. Sylvia and Christabel offer opposing views of their childhood; Christabel painted Sylvia as emotionally fragile and incurably shy, whilst Sylvia was wholly aware of the preference Emmeline had for her eldest daughter and resented the lack of attention and nurture she received from her mother. Instead, Sylvia formed a close and loving bond with her father. She later wrote of him:

'Our father, vilified and boycotted, yet beloved by a multitude of people in many walks of life, was a standard-bearer for every forlorn hope, every unpopular yet worthy cause then conceived for the uplifting of oppressed and suffering humanity.'

The early death of Richard would have a lasting effect on Sylvia. She would revere him without fault or hesitation and carry with her his dedication and commitment to the working classes and to a socialist future for the rest of her life.

Sylvia attended Manchester High School for Girls alongside Christabel and Adela. Sylvia's artistic achievements won her first a place at the Manchester School of Art, then at the Royal College of Art. Determined to carve a career as an artist, Sylvia said of her chosen path later in life:

'I would decorate the halls where people would foregather in the movement to win the new world, and make banners for the meetings and processions.'

She got her wish, as the photograph of her painting the shop sign shows. In 1900, the Pankhurst Memorial Hall opened in Broughton, Salford, built with funds raised by the leader of the Independent Labour Party, Keir Hardie and the party's secretary, Ramsay Macdonald. Sylvia was commissioned to decorate the interior. Three years later, her artistry would be called upon once more, as the start of a movement that would define her public, private, and familial life, was about to begin.

After the death of Richard Pankhurst, the family moved out of Victoria Park to 62 Nelson Street, where, after Emmeline's frustrations with the National Union of Women's Suffrage Societies and the lack of support of the Independent Labour Party led to Emmeline, Christabel and Sylvia founding the Women's Social and Political Union. Sylvia wrote and published two accounts of the women's suffrage movement throughout her life, offering a unique insight into those early days of the WSPU. She wrote of that momentous night:

'Almost all the women who were present on that original occasion were working women, members of the Labour movement, but it was decided from the first that the Union should be entirely independent of Class or Party.'

Sylvia's was determined for it to be known that the WSPU was being founded by working women and women linked to the Independent Labour Party. This is telling of the sort of women's movement she strived for, one that, ultimately, the WSPU would not offer. Despite this, in the early days of the WSPU, Sylvia played a crucial role. In 1905, after Christabel and Annie Kenney were arrested after disrupting a Liberal meeting at the Free Trade Hall in Manchester, the WSPU gained more traction. Being in a key location in London, Sylvia was able to support her mother firstly in lobbying Parliament and, until Emmeline moved to the capital, organising the movement.

Whilst first working as an unpaid WSPU organiser, Sylvia was made the honourary secretary of the WSPU, and with her mother's sister Mary Clarke and WSPU organiser Annie Kenney, formed a London branch of the organisation. From her lodgings in Kensington, Sylvia hosted committee meetings and organised open-air meetings. On February 1906, the opening of Parliament, Sylvia organised an open-air meeting in Trafalgar Square, at which Keir Hardie, Emmeline Pankhurst, early suffragist Elizabeth Wolstenholme-Elmy and Annie Kenney all spoke. Over four hundred men and women turned up to show their support.

When Christabel finished her Law degree in Manchester, Sylvia resigned from her leadership post, conscious she had only been in the role temporarily whilst the elder sister completed her studies. Christabel moved to London and Sylvia took on a secondary role. Again, as she had once hoped, Sylvia used art to create the banners and symbols that would define a movement. Sylvia designed many pamphlets and designs used by WSPU, including the iconic angel of freedom. When the militant action of the organisation was amplified, she designed the Holloway brooch, that was presented to suffragettes who had been incarcerated at Holloway Gaol. In its design, Sylvia reclaimed the prison arrow.

As the WSPU grew in membership and in strength, Sylvia became more and more conflicted and isolated from Emmeline and Christabel. Although Sylvia was dedicated to the militant movement, she felt it was moving away from supporting working-class women and that the leadership of her mother and sister was becoming too autocratic. Sylvia had always been different from Emmeline and Christabel and it had always been apparent that Christabel was Emmeline's favourite daughter. Now this private favouritism had made its way into the movement that Sylvia had helped build and had fought so passionately for. Like many others who dared to challenge the iron rule of Emmeline and Christabel, Sylvia would soon suffer the consequences.

'You are unreasonable, always have been, and I fear, always will be. I suppose you were made so!'

Sylvia received these words in a letter from her mother in 1914. Family tensions had long been building, as Sylvia's politics were moving further and further away from those of her sister and mother. Sylvia found an outlet for her socialist politics and her dedication to working women, through the East London Federation, a branch of the WSPU that still used militant tactics to campaign for the vote. Several boroughs of East London united under the flag of the ELF and it was here that Sylvia carried out some of her best and most fulfilling work. Whilst the WSPU were solely focused on winning the vote, Sylvia worked hard for other causes, championing working rights, food halls and shelter for vulnerable women.

Her work with the ELF was the final straw for Emmeline and Christabel. The ELF had evolved into a democratic and active organisation of its own, something the Pankhursts would not tolerate. Public political clashes between the sisters only heightened these tensions. Sylvia was a supporter of Home Rule in Ireland, supporting nationalists on strike in Dublin, something Christabel had publicly condemned.

In 1914, after over a decade of gruelling, painful and life-consuming campaigning, Sylvia was called to Paris, where Christabel was living. Whilst there, it was decided that Sylvia's ELF must split from the WSPU and become its own campaigning organisation. Sylvia's relationship with her mother and sister was damaged beyond repair. After a lifetime of craving her mother's pride and affection, this was the final blow and the push for Sylvia to finally turn her back on the WSPU and fully embrace her socialist calling.

The ELF changed its name to the East End Federation of Suffragettes and continued to use public, militant campaigning to lobby for the vote. In June 1914, a deputation of East End working women went to Downing Street. Although Sylvia had only recently been released from prison under the terms of the 1913 Cat and Mouse Act, she too travelled to Westminster, awaiting the outcome. Asquith accepted the deputation of six working-class women, whilst Sylvia waited with the crowds outside. Asquith promised to give the matter of women's suffrage careful and considerate support and the deputation was seen as a victory for the suffragettes. Asquith's promises, however, were made redundant only weeks later.

On 4th August 1914, the First World War broke out and the country was thrown into turmoil. The suffragists and the suffragettes had to choose a side. Sylvia, ever different, ever defiant of her family, chose to fight for peace; Emmeline and Christabel shook hands with the Government and ended their campaigns for women's suffrage.

Sylvia did not stop campaigning during the war. She wrote to James Middleton, secretary of the War Emergency Workers' Committee, to offer the assistance of the ELFS in supporting working-class women during the war – the offer was rejected. Sylvia began to emerge as a thorn in the government's side, as she staunchly opposed the war and fanatically campaigned against it.

Again, this line of action came from her socialist values. Sylvia was devastated that Emmeline and Christabel, in her eyes, were betraying the legacy of Richard Pankhurst, who had been staunchly anti-war. As she drifted further away from her family, Sylvia relied on the love and support from the relationships she had forged through her political campaigns.

Like many Independent Labour Party supporters, Sylvia supported adult suffrage – the vote for all men and women aged 21 and over. As the war divided many of the suffragists and suffragettes, many of her old comrades returned to campaign alongside Sylvia, including Emmeline Pethwick-Lawrence. As Sylvia supported strikes in the East End and used her newspaper, *The Dreadnought*, to release anti-war articles, she suffered a terrible personal loss in 1915 when Keir Hardie, the former leader of the Labour Party, passed away. Sylvia and Keir were close friends and almost certainly embroiled in a love affair. He had guided and supported her throughout her many campaigns and sat in vigil at her bedside as she had recovered from force-feeding. His death was a devastating blow.

After the war, Sylvia travelled to communist Russia after the revolution and continued to use the *Dreadnought* to offer a left-leaning perspective on social and political issues. The newspaper was outspoken on issues such as the Russian Revolution, Irish Home Rule, racism and anti-Semitism. 1n 1920, she became the first editor to employ a black journalist, when Claude Mackay joined the paper.

Her fight against fascism drew her attention to the cause of Ethiopia. Unlike her sister Christabel, Sylvia despised the Italian dictator Mussolini. Her partner, Silvio Cario, was an Italian anarchist who opposed Mussolini and worked closely with Italian anti-fascists in London. When Mussolini and his Italian forces invaded Ethiopia in 1935, Sylvia began a campaign for the British government to recognise and defy Mussolini's invasion, especially their use of gas against the Ethiopian forces. She set up the newspaper, the New Time and Ethiopia News and through this platform lobbied for change.

Sylvia had become more detached from Emmeline and Christabel since the end of the First World War. In 1927, the bond between mother and daughter was broken forever when Sylvia gave birth to hers and Silvo's son, Richard Keir Pethwick Pankhurst. Emmeline never forgave her for breaking the social norm like this and they did not speak again. In 1954, after years of supporting Ethiopia and after the death of Silvio, Sylvia and Richard moved to Ethiopia, where she died in 1960.

Like her mother and sisters, Sylvia remained an agitator of the government for the rest of her life. Despite growing up in the shadows of her bolder sisters and formidable mother, Sylvia carved her own path in life by staying true to her socialist values, by giving a voice to working-class women and fighting fascism. She will go down in history as one of the bravest and most principled suffragettes.

EMMELINE PANKHURST

Walking through St Peter's Square in Manchester, a statue now stands by the tram stop, surrounded by office buildings. Every day, people walk past the bronze sculpture of Emmeline Pankhurst standing on a chair, her arm outstretched, her expression moving as if she is there, encouraging the crowds to take action. Some days, flowers are tucked into the hand, in the colours of her campaign: green, white and purple. It now seems almost impossible that any other woman would have been voted to be immortalised in bronze. Emmeline Pankhurst, though her name may have faded in and out of fashion, has never been forgotten by the city that made her and her campaign. The statue is not the only memorial to Emmeline in the city. Only a short walk down Oxford Road, the Pankhurst Centre sits nestled by the Manchester Royal Infirmary, the home where she lived with her children, saved by campaigners in the 1980s from demolition. The sitting room where Emmeline and her daughters founded the Women's Social and Political Union (WSPU) is now made up to look as it had done over a hundred years ago, when a small group of women gathered there to join Mrs Pankhurst's ranks.

Emmeline's story has never been forgotten, nor faded into history. As she was the face and voice of the militant suffragette movement, so she was the face of the centenary celebrations of the Representation of the People Act in 2018. Her famous motto, 'deeds not words', has been echoed not only across Manchester, but across the world. Indeed, she lived her entire life by these words; before 1903, before the WSPU, she was already taking up action for the causes that mattered to her. Whilst she remains famous for leading the militant campaign for the vote, Emmeline's life has more flesh on the bone – before and after.

Emmeline was, and is, a contentious figure. Her support of the First World War and her later leanings towards more radical politics sometimes mar the view we have of her. But Emmeline Pankhurst was not a hero, or a saint. She was a flawed woman, but a real woman, and we must celebrate and acknowledge her for what she did for the liberation of women, for fighting almost to the point of death for suffrage and for political freedom.

When looking back at her childhood, both through her own recollections in her autobiography *My Own Story* and records left behind, Emmeline could have been raised for revolution. She was born Emmeline Goulden, to Robert and Jane Goulden, on 14th July 1858 – Bastille Day, a day of revolution. Her birth certificate contradicts this, stating she was born on the 15th, but it suited Emmeline to believe she shared a birthday with such a significant anniversary of rebellion. Her mother was from the Isle of Man, the first place in the British Isles to give women the vote, and her father ran a calico and bleach works in Salford.

Illustration by **Nell Smith**

Her family were from radical stock; Emmeline's grandfather had been in the crowd at Peterloo. The eldest of ten children, Emmeline was favoured by her father because of her talent for reading, although it rankled when her parents watched her sleep one night and proclaimed: *'What a pity she wasn't born a lad.'* Despite their support for suffrage, this was Emmeline's first lesson in gender inequality. Still, her parents encouraged her education and shared their interest with reform.

Like Emmeline would one day do with her own children, Emmeline's mother encouraged her to be active at meetings. Sophia Goulden took Emmeline and her siblings to Abolitionist meetings, where they collected pennies for freed slaves in America. She attended her first suffrage meeting at the age of fourteen, when she saw Lydia Becker speak in Manchester. Emmeline recalled this event clearly in her autobiography, stating:

'I left the meeting a conscious and confirmed suffragist.'

Emmeline finished her education at a school in her beloved Paris, the home of revolution, where she shared a room with Noemie Rochefort, the daughter of a radical journalist Henri Rochefort. It was here that Emmeline became enamoured with radical action and republicanism and would stay friends with Noemie for the rest of her life. Her love of France never left her and she adopted a sense of fashion, culture and style from her time in Paris that she would never lose; indeed, she once proclaimed that Richard was different from every other Englishman, the only explanation was that he must possess ancestral French blood. On her return to Manchester three years later, Emmeline would bring with her not only these new fashions, but these political values, fired by the Rochefort connections she had made. Returning to Manchester, Emmeline almost instantly began working towards social and political change in the city. This energetic and charming young woman was not content with helping to run the Goulden household, however, and soon she would meet the man who would make a formidable and loyal partner in political campaigning: Dr Richard Pankhurst.

Emmeline at the time was campaigning for the Married Women's Property Act (which Richard had written) and was regularly attending suffrage meetings in the city. Richard Pankhurst had been one of the fiercest campaigners in the city for the enfranchisement of women and it was no surprise that their paths soon crossed. Emmeline wanted to step outside of the family bonds and live her own life – Richard, who saw her as an equal, would help her achieve this. Their relationship was founded on a shared sense of justice, but there's no denying their love and devotion to each other. Sylvia Pankhurst, her daughter, writes of the meeting of her parents as something out of a classical romance novel; Emmeline, the young, beautiful woman, and Richard, a scholar whom the entire city admired (in Sylvia's recollections), and who should have barely noticed her; Sylvia writes:

'She thought he would regard her only as an ignorant child; she, an ill-educated girl of twenty, he twice her age, a distinguished scholar…yet with her svelte figure, her beautiful violet blue eyes, her clear olive skin with the warm flush to her cheeks, her jet black hair, and those perfectly arched, finely pencilled black eyebrows, that golden voice…that indefinable and never failing charm she bore all her life; she was lovely enough to win the heart of any man.'

They were married in 1879 and moved to Drayton Terrace in Trafford, where their first two children, Christabel Harriette and Estelle Sylvia were born. As Emmeline noted in her autobiography, Richard did not want a wife turned into a domestic machine and Emmeline balanced her duties as a mother whilst still serving on the executive committee of the Manchester Women's Suffrage Society. Mary Jane Goulden, Emmeline's sister, lived with the family and would be looked upon by the Pankhurst children as a second mother. A dispute with the Goulden family after her father had refused to bestow property on Emmeline, resulted in the once close and cordial relationship between the Pankhursts and the Gouldens ending abruptly.

Emmeline had campaigned every time Richard had stood for election in Manchester, first in 1883, where he stood as an independent candidate. His radical agenda, including Irish Home Rule and women's suffrage, was unpopular; his opponent also spent over three times as much as he had done in his campaign. Emmeline had, on Richard's behalf, asked Lydia Becker to advocate for her husband; due to old disagreements, Lydia had refused. It was perhaps Emmeline's first exposure to the ruthless tactics used in the political arena and the knowledge that justice and loyalty rarely prevailed.

Emmeline believed that Richard would have a better chance of gaining a seat in the House of Commons and becoming a Member of Parliament if the family relocated to London. And so, with an ambition to gain economic freedoms of her own, Emmeline lead the family to London, where they rented at first a house and then shop on Hampstead Road. The shop was named Emerson & Co, selling elegant and fashionable house furnishings. It didn't prosper as she had hoped and throughout their time in the capital, the shop moved home not once but twice, still never quite achieving the success that Emmeline had hoped for. The family's financial situation was rarely one of comfort, but they always got by.

Wealthy they were not, but the Pankhursts were rich in their company. In London, they were close to the centre of the socialist web and took part in meetings and protests. Emmeline had lent her support and her help to the Match Girls' Strike of 1888, one of the first organised strikes carried out by working women at the Bryant and May match factory. Richard continued to advocate for the political and social freedoms of the working class, offering legal aid across the country. It was at Hampstead Road that Emmeline suffered a major personal blow, when her four year old son, Frank, contracted dysentery and died soon after Emmeline had returned from visiting Richard in Manchester. Emmeline never truly recovered from his death; she would often speak of him and only on the birth of Harry ten months later did she appear to recover from the tragedy. This event was not without terror itself. Emmeline suffered severe haemorrhaging moments after giving birth and survived solely due to the quick actions of the children's nurse, Susannah, who ran out and found a doctor to care for her. These experiences of loss, and simply the horrors of childbirth, would perhaps encourage her long-lasting and fierce empathy with the young women she would meet in her job as a birth and deaths registrar, later in life.

Soon after Frank's death, the family relocated to 8 Russell Square, where the family home was decorated almost as a showroom for Emerson's; Sylvia remembers Persian rugs, oriental furnishings, and William Morris-esque patterns around the house, creating a sumptuous and exotic ambience. It isn't hard to picture the middle-class socialists of the day gathering to discuss reform and revolution in such a dramatic and unorthodox environment. Sylvia describes their guests at 8 Russell Square as:

'Fabians, Anarchists, Suffragists, Free Thinkers, Radicals and Humanitarians of all schools.'

These radicals included Tom Mann, William Garrison, Annie Besant and William Morris, whom Emmeline believed to be prejudiced against her for her Parisian style of dress. It would be here, amongst these comrades, that Emmeline's name became well-spoken and well-known as an agitator for women's suffrage. Indeed, not long after Harry's birth, in the living room of the house, the Women's Franchise League (WFL) was founded, differing from the National Suffrage Societies, led by the formidable Lydia Becker, by refusing to compromise on married women not being able to vote, as was being suggested. As the WFL fought for equality in divorce, marriage and enfranchisement, Sylvia Pankhurst recalls the cry against the league, as: 'Half a loaf is better than no bread!' It is a little ironic that Emmeline would have rallied so strongly against this, when in 1918, she perceived the partial enfranchisement of women as a victory.

Richard had failed to win an election again, this time in London and by the winter of 1892, it became clear their financial situation was no longer suited to the capital city. Emerson's was a financial failure and huge repair costs on the Russell Square house at the end of its lease was the last straw for the family. They moved first to Southport, then Disley, before settling back in their home city of Manchester, in the leafy, elegant suburb of Victoria Park. It was as if London had been an exotic dream, where the Pankhursts had been, if possible, fervently radicalised to the left, further than they had leant before. In Manchester, Emmeline became a Poor Law Guardian and once again Richard stood for election in the city, this time in Gorton as an ILP candidate. Although he failed once more, the socialist spirit of the Pankhurst family did not falter. When the ILP were banned from hosting open-air meetings at Boggart Hole Clough, both Richard and Emmeline fervently fought against it; Richard defended those who were arrested, including Emmeline, protesting the right for free speech. Emmeline emerged here as a presence to be reckoned with for one of the first times; a powerful public speaker and entirely unafraid of arrest or retribution.

Emmeline is often remembered, most especially in Sylvia's memoirs, as not particularly maternal (like most middle-class women, Emmeline wasn't always required to be so, having the support of nursemaids and governesses for the most part of her children's upbringing). Her bond with Christabel however, was undeniably strong and it was out of concern for her smart but somewhat directionless daughter that they embarked on their European travels in the summer of 1898, leaving Sylvia at home to look after the household. Richard, whose health had been ailing for some time, refused to let Sylvia call a doctor. He sent a telegram to Emmeline asking her to return, but by the time she stepped off the train from London, the news of Richard's death greeted her on the back of a fellow passenger's newspaper. Emmeline had lost her greatest love, the person who she had built a radical and adoring life with. The inscription on his headstone was a quote from American poet Walt Whitman, reading:

'Faithful and true and my ever-loving comrade'

The family moved to 62 Nelson Street, a smaller house closer to the centre of Manchester. Emmeline could not wallow in her grief, for Richard's death had left the family finances in a precarious state. She took on the role of birth and deaths registrar and re-opened Emerson's on King Street to try and bring in more money.

The role of birth and death registrar opened Emmeline's eyes to some of the worst poverty and female inequality in Manchester, as she wrote in her autobiography:

'It was touching to see how glad women were to have a women registrar…I was shocked to be reminded over and over again of the little respect there was in the world for women and children.'

Emmeline was met with women who had spent their entire adult life between childbirth and mill work; young women who had been raped, unmarried and mistreated. She was reminded almost constantly of the horrors that women without a vote, a voice, or any political representation, faced.

We will never know what Emmeline was feeling as she addressed the women in her parlour on October 10th 1903. What breaking point had she reached? What exhaustion, anger, frustration? And was there hope? Did she truly believe this small formation would be the final, decade-long push needed to secure some women the vote? From that quiet moment of rebellion, Emmeline was setting a course for her own life to change forever, from her political leanings to her relationships with her children. Did she know she was to sacrifice her mental and physical health? The answer, of course, is no. She cannot have known what was to follow. What is clear, however, is that she was prepared to do anything to win the vote, on the terms that she and her late husband had felt achievable. The relationship with the ILP, however, would not last. The Pankhurst Memorial Hall, built to commemorate Richard, housed a branch of the ILP that banned women from their meetings and later refused to support women's suffrage whilst the property qualification remained in place. This split would never be reconciled.

Emmeline's compelling and refreshing manner drew women to the WSPU and the organisation began to grow. Despite constant travel to London and lobbying Members of Parliament, it was 1905, when Christabel and Annie Kenney were arrested at the Liberal meeting in the Free Trade Hall, that inspired a national outcry. Emmeline began to travel around the country delivering talks, moving permanently to London to be closer to parliament.

For the next fifteen years, the WSPU would dominate the campaign for women's suffrage, with Emmeline at the helm. If she was considered the general, then she indeed built up an army of devoted soldiers. From the London Headquarters in Lincoln's Inn, Emmeline and Christabel, alongside WSPU stalwarts and financiers, Emmeline and Fredrick Pethwick-Lawrence, organised the movement that would surge across the nation. Emmeline led everything, from meetings and talks delivered around the country, to the first lobbies against the government for the vote. She was first arrested in 1908 after storming parliament with several other WSPU members.

These actions continued as the government repeatedly denied women the right to vote. After the first women went on hunger strike (and were subsequently force-fed), Emmeline spoke out about the horrific conditions in gaol and celebrations were held for women who were released from prison and presented with the Holloway brooch designed by Sylvia. In the same year, Emmeline took a tour of America, delivering lectures on the question of suffrage. Emmeline suffered further loss on her return when her only son, Harry, passed away. She could not know that in the same year, her sister and closest companion would also pass away, from injuries inflicted on the infamous Black Friday in 1910, where a deputation of three-hundred suffragettes were brutally attacked by police officers, in uniform and plain clothes, as they attempted to reach parliament.

The WSPU's militant action ramped up as the government pushed back furiously against enfranchisement for women and Emmeline became their number one target. She was arrested and imprisoned after leading the now notorious window smashing campaigns, arguing: 'Better broken windows than broken promises.' Emmeline was never force fed, for fear she would become the campaigns greatest martyr. She became an expert of illusiveness, often escaping to Paris to stay with Christabel. Loyal WSPU members, or 'bodyguards', helped with these escapes. What became clear, year after year, is that the campaign would never weaken; it was only a matter of time before the violence would cause the government irreparable damage.

At the outbreak of the First World War, a turning point arrived for the WSPU. Emmeline met with her one-time political nemesis, Lloyd George, and put patriotism above enfranchisement. Emmeline and Christabel suspended all militant activity and changed the name of The Suffragette to The Britannia. This caused a huge split between both suffragists and suffragettes. Those who believed in peace, who thought that to stop the campaign would be a betrayal to everything that had been fought for before. Emmeline and Christabel helped to enlist young men and encouraged conscription. They organised marches to enlist women workers into the factory and munitions roles. Emmeline adopted four young girls – orphaned in war – and encouraged other suffragettes to do the same.

When, on the 6th February 1918, the Representation of the People Act was passed, everything that Emmeline had been fighting for came into fruition, but in true Emmeline fashion, her campaigning did not come to an end. She formed the Women's Party out of the loyal WSPU members, preparing women to step into their new roles as enfranchised active citizens in the next election. When in November that year Parliament passed an act that enabled women to become MPs, Emmeline was determined that Christabel would be the first female MP and was devastated when she was defeated by the Labour candidate. She moved to Canada with her four adoptive daughters and lectured on the dangers of Venereal Diseases. Although revered on both sides of the Atlantic, Emmeline couldn't find a cause that stirred her as suffrage had.

With the support of Christabel, Emmeline moved back to the United Kingdom and settled in London. In 1925, she unsuccessfully ran as the Conservative candidate in Whitechapel. Cared for by her dedicated daughter Christabel, Emmeline's health continued to fail, and in 1928 she passed away in a nursing home, just before her 70th birthday. Years of physical and emotional toil from the most important fight for women in British history had worn away at her strength. At her funeral, hundreds of suffragettes, led by Christabel and Sylvia, followed her coffin into St John's Church, Westminster. The minister summarised her life well, saying:

'We salute her as an heroic leader, we acclaim her as a friend, and we respect her as a wise counsellor. We owe her a deep debt of gratitude which we can best discharge by carrying on still farther the cause to which she gave her life.'

Emmeline did give her life to the campaign. Although she wasn't the first in the fight, Emmeline will go down in history as one of the most powerful, passionate and inspirational leaders of the 20th century.

The Journey

I was elected to Manchester City Council in May 2011 representing Didsbury East and the Labour Party.

In March 2014 I was having coffee with my good friend Anne-Marie Glennon in the Sculpture Hall in the Town Hall. She looked at the busts surrounding us and exclaimed:

"These are all men! Where are the women?"

In late May 2014 the Labour Group on Manchester City Council held its Annual General Meeting. The usual ballot took place for backbench members of the group to have the chance to address the Council. If their name came out of the bag they could then propose any resolution they liked for discussion at a City Council meeting - provided it didn't cost the City Council any money!

Old Moat Councillor Suzannah Reeves' name was first out. She would present her resolution at the Full City Council meeting on Wednesday 30th July. Sitting just below me in the Council Chamber she let out a cry of exasperation. *"Oh no, I can't. I'm on holiday!"*

Her chance gone, the next name out was mine. I knew exactly what I was going to talk about. Determined not to let my complete ignorance of how to commission a statue project get in the way, I wrote the resolution.

We would create a statue of a woman of significance to Manchester .

Dave Godfrey was the obvious first port of call. Dave has wide ranging experience having worked in the City Council Leader's Office for many years. With trepidation I asked him to take a quick look over the statue resolution wording. Dave smiled as he absorbed the contents. At that point Leader Sir Richard Leese walked in and Dave passed him the sheet of paper suggesting he take a look too.

Richard was enthusiastic from that moment and said that Ardwick born 'Red' Ellen Wilkinson should be considered for the statue. In the back of my mind Ellen was already a potential candidate having been one of the instigators of the 1936 Jarrow March.

Journalist Jennifer Williams' enthusiastic endorsement of the statue idea in the Manchester Evening News meant that I was soon receiving many more suggestions for who should be honoured. Doctor Ali Ronan from Manchester Metropolitan University suggested Margaret Ashton, the first female Councillor in Manchester. Elizabeth Raffald, a remarkable eighteenth century businesswoman, was championed by Suze Appleton. The suggestions continued to arrive until I had twenty names. Striking a balance amongst this long-list was to be an important consideration. I had telling conversations with my fellow Councillors, the late Sheila Newman and Amina Lone, who championed the need for greater diversity on the list.

On Wednesday 30th July 2014, Manchester City Council gave its unanimous support for the idea of the statue of 'a woman of significance to Manchester'. In my speech to the Council, I pledged to cycle from Lands End to John O'Groats to raise awareness and money for the campaign. I would do so in twenty stages, each one devoted to one of the women being considered.

On 28th May 2015, in front of over a hundred people at the Central Library Performance space the Lord Mayor, Councillor Paul Murphy, joined me to host the unveiling of the twenty names. One by one the presenters gave their minute long speeches in support of their favoured candidate. The Lord Mayor then drew a number out of the hat representing the day of the ride that they would be honoured.

Eight young women from Levenshulme High School talked about Louise Da-Cocodia, whilst Matthew Frost presented the facts on Kathleen Ollerenshaw. Thirteen-year-old Emily Dodd made the case for Emmeline Pankhurst, and Abby Robinson passionately championed Emily Williamson. Sisters Eve and Mia Gilmour, represented Christabel Pankhurst. Helen Freeborough made the case for Enriqueta Rylands. A letter of endorsement from the Leader of South Tyneside Council, Iain Malcolm, was read out talking about Ellen Wilkinson.'

I devoted June 2015 to the Lands End to John O'Groats cycle ride.

▲ *Andrew about to leave Lands End; 3rd June 2015*

Most LEJOG groups aim to complete the ride in eight to twelve days and simply head up the western side of England to the Scottish border by the most direct route. I had the advantage that I was cycling alone for the most part and could choose my own timings and itinerary. I bought Ordnance Survey maps covering the entire route and over the course of many happy hours in the Fletcher Moss pub in Didsbury planned my journey using quiet country roads where possible.

My good friends Tom and Penny Tomie accompanied me on the first four days of the route. They drove carrying my luggage. St Michael's Mount was my last sight of the sea for a thousand miles.

▲ *St Michael's Mount, Cornwall; 3rd June 2015*

Climbing Dartmoor in the fog without lights was a nerve-wracking experience. The Somerset levels with Glastonbury Tor in the distance were a welcome highlight as the cycling became easier.

Andrew tackles Dartmoor in the fog;
5th June 2015 (credit; Ian 'Tom' Tomie) ▼

Ann Platt took over as my accompanying friend for the four days from Shepton Mallet to Manchester. In Leek, I had some very welcome friends join me in the saddle for an excellent day's cycling via my home turf of the Manifold Valley and the Cat & Fiddle. Dave Godfrey, Paul Gilmour, Pete Dodd and Dave Gater were all fresh and made me realise how tired I was!

We were welcomed into Albert Square by many of my fellow Councillors and Jeff Smith, MP for Manchester Withington. After a day of rest I set off again, in the rain, with Dave Godfrey. We tackled a Bradley Wiggins training climb north of Colne and spent the night in Skipton.

▲ *Uschi and Davy Iredale with Andrew in the*
Yorkshire Dales; 14th June 2015

My new travelling companions were Uschi and Davy Iredale who would now stick with me to John O'Groats. The route took in The Yorkshire Dales before arriving at Jarrow on the banks of the Tyne. Iain Malcolm, the local Council leader, arranged a civic reception for us.

▲ *Andrew with the Jarrow Crusade Memorial; 15th June 2015*

Strong winds and heavy construction traffic on the run into Edinburgh made for the most perilous cycling conditions yet. Paul and Pete joined me again as we headed over the Forth Road Bridge. On we travelled via Glencoe to Fort William. General Wade's Military Road is a stand out piece of military engineering high above Loch Ness.

Andrew reaches John O'Groats after twenty days in the saddle covering 1,059 miles; 26th June 2015

▶

▲ *General Wade's Military Road running high above Loch Ness; 22nd June 2015*

From Inverness, good cycle routes were mixed in with the terror of the A9 in heavy fog and fast moving vehicles.

I arrived at John O'Groats on Friday, 26th June. I resisted the temptation to throw my bike into the sea.

It had been a journey of 1,059 miles over twenty day-long stages.

In the autumn of 2015 I assessed the merits of the twenty women. How much support had they received on their day in the spotlight? Could a balanced shortlist be created?

In October the shortlist went live to the public and the response was immediate. For the next two months thousands of people voted from across the world. At the January 2016 Council meeting, during the Lord Mayor's special business, I announced the result. Emmeline Pankhurst had won by a landslide. In the public gallery the Chief Executive of the Pankhurst Centre, Gail Heath, unveiled her 'Votes for Women' sash and enthusiastically declared her support.'

On 18th July 2016 I hosted a briefing for potential sculptors alongside Emmeline's Great Grand Daughter, Dr Helen Pankhurst. Helen presented her vision for the statue. It would, she said, be a rallying point for future meetings of women in the city. I explained to the eighteen sculptors gathered there that six would be shortlisted. Each would receive £5,000 to create a 40 cm high bronze maquette of their design for the statue. The successful sculptor would also agree to create a limited edition of twelve similar maquettes for sale.

A few weeks later interviews were conducted to find our shortlist. Designs of all kinds were presented to the newly-formed Emmeline Pankhurst Statue Selection Committee. Members of the Committee included myself, Helen, Councillor Sarah Judge, Lead Member for Women on Manchester City Council, Amanda Wallace, Deputy Director of Manchester Art Gallery, Louise Sutherland, Chair of the Pankhurst Centre, Keir McGuinness, Trustee of the Public Monuments and Sculptures Association and Councillor Luthfur Rahman, Executive Member for Leisure and Arts on the City Council.

The six-strong shortlist contained three men and three women, one working with her father.

On 27th February 2017, the six designs were unveiled. Jeff Smith, MP, hosted the event in Portcullis House, part of the Houses of Parliament. There then followed a question and answer session with the sculptors at HOME in Manchester, an exhibition of the designs in the Council Chamber ante-room and a display in the sculpture hall. On March 9th 2017, two hundred people attended a fundraising dinner with the sculptors at the Radisson Blu Edwardian Hotel, once the Free Trade Hall.

▲ *Lord Mayor Councillor Carl Austin-Behan with Hazel Reeves and her design 'Rise Up Women'*

For the rest of the month the designs went on display at Manchester Art Gallery where a further two thousand people visited to see them and vote.

▲ *Andrew with the shortlisted designs at Manchester Art Gallery; 14th March 2017*

On 31st March 2017, I sat down to make the difficult calls to the sculptors. Only one could be successful. At 11.00 a.m. on the morning of Tuesday 4th April 2017 the winner was announced. Hazel Reeves and her design 'Rise Up Women' was the popular choice of the voting public and the unanimous selection of the interview panel.

Hazel Reeves won the competition because her design captured the imagination of those who saw it. The simplicity of 'Rise Up Women' lay at its heart. Emmeline stands, mouth open in mid-speech, atop an ordinary household chair. This makeshift stage was a regular feature of suffragette meetings. Her right arm is outstretched towards the crowd. At one and a quarter life size the statue is also designed to be accessible. The space between the meeting circle and the statue is sufficient for anyone in a wheelchair to manoeuvre around the statue viewing it from all angles at close range.

Hazel's previous public designs include the railway locomotive engineer Sir Nigel Gresley at Kings Cross station in London and The Cracker Packers in Carlisle. This portrays two female workers from different eras at the Carrs Biscuit Factory there.

As I was to find, funding the statue was one of the most difficult parts of the project. This has been borne out by the number of conversations I have had since, with campaigns across the country all championing their own female icon. For all of us, raising the money was and is the big sticking point. Edwina Wolstencroft had bought the first of the maquettes and over the next eighteen months others came forward as gold sponsors to purchase the rest of the limited edition. Manchester Airport Group were the first of the corporate funders for the statue, closely followed by Property Alliance Group.

Hazel hands over the first maquette to Edwina Wolstencroft; 5th April 2017 ▼

My twenty days cycling from Lands End to John O'Groats had raised three thousand pounds. With some good connections and calls I raised many times that figure with much less effort!

On 8th March 2017, Chancellor of the Exchequer Philip Hammond rose in the House of Commons to announce his budget. The Government would make five million pounds available for celebrations of the one hundredth anniversary of women securing the vote in 1918. By the time the Chancellor had sat down, I had emailed him outlining the Emmeline Pankhurst statue project and making a request to meet. I had also noticed that the television cameras had gone to Justine Greening, then Education Secretary, as the announcement was made. For good measure, I emailed her too.

A few weeks later, on 23rd April, I received an email from an official in the Government Equalities Office. The project was of interest. Over the coming weeks discussions continued. In one interesting exchange I challenged the official on the fact that the Millicent Fawcett statue in London was to receive one million of the five million pounds allocated to the celebrations. *"Ah well, you see, that's a national project. Yours is in Manchester."*

Showing that this London centric view could be successfully challenged became an unspoken aim for the statue campaign.

On 26th May 2017, representatives from the GEO arrived in Manchester. The GEO officials had asked if I could organise a meeting where they met local women's groups. Later that day, over lunch at the offices of accountancy firm Mazars, the meeting took place and the various groups represented had the opportunity to make a bid for GEO funding. I went on to introduce the GEO senior official to newly appointed City Council Chief Executive Joanne Roney. Meanwhile, her GEO colleagues visited The Pankhurst Centre.

The City Council would go on to successfully submit a joint bid on behalf of The Pankhurst Centre and the statue campaign for funding.

Securing the Government funding meant that the unveiling of the statue could be brought forward to 2018. Other planned fundraising activities could be put to one side

February 6th 2018 marked the one hundredth anniversary of the passing of the Act giving some women the vote. To celebrate, Prime Minister Theresa May visited The Pankhurst Centre and met Dr Helen Pankhurst and me. She saw the design of the statue for herself. Later in the spring, the statue of suffragist Millicent Fawcett was unveiled in Parliament Square, Westminster. I attended and gained some valuable insights into how best to unveil the statue of Emmeline.

▲ *Prime Minister Theresa May visits The Pankhurst Centre to see the statue design and to meet Helen Pankhurst; 6th February 2018*

The siting of the statue in St Peter's Square would effectively complete the public realm works in what is now a magnificent space.

The planning consultancy firm Turley had generously agreed to provide their expertise pro bono. Over the course of several meetings and conference calls with Hazel Reeves, Bob May, their director, and colleague Peter Rowe, the detailed planning application soon came together. On Thursday 8th February 2018, the Planning Committee met in the Town Hall Council Chamber. The statue application was on the agenda.

▲ *Fatima Shahid in the Council Chamber; 8th February 2018*

▲ *Bob May and Peter Rowe of Turley; 21st June 2017*

As applicant, I deferred my right to speak to Fatima Shahid, an eleven-year-old pupil from Newall Green Primary School in Wythenshawe. I had been introduced to Fatima by my fellow Councillor Mary Monaghan who worked at the school. Fatima spoke beautifully and the meeting attendees, more used to hard bitten discussions about contentious planning applications, gave her a big round of applause. The committee endorsed the application unanimously.

The legalities were completed. Sarah Walton, Partner at Weightmans, again acting pro-bono, drew up the formal agreement with Hazel Reeves.

Sarah Walton, Partner at Weightmans, with the maquette; 30th August 2017 ▼

Hazel at work on the statue armature ▶

On 13th June 2018, I led a party of visitors to see her. Fellow Councillors Sarah Judge, Julie Reid, Sam Lynch, Joan Davies and Lee-Ann Igbon came on the trip along with Heidi and Lisa, members of the Wythenshawe-based Safe Spots group and guest Julia Baker-Smith. Hazel showed us progress on the statue so far, answered questions and explained the 'lost wax' statue process.'

Councillors and Safe Spots volunteers ▲
at Hazel's studio; 13th June 2018

A key element of Hazel's' design is the white Portland stone meeting circle that would surround the statue. At the meeting with sculptors in July 2016, Hazel had noted the surrounding buildings and the nearby water feature. All were in white stone and a significant reason for Hazel's design being chosen was the simplicity of the circle design.

On 14th June 2018 I travelled to Corfe Castle in Dorset, to visit the Lovell Stone Quarry where the stone for the meeting circle was being quarried. It was also being carved into the curved blocks ahead of the journey north.

Hazel had worked with Jeremy Tilley of Tilley Stonemasons on other projects and it would be his team that would install the meeting circle.

Another key consideration was what lay beneath the proposed site in St Peter's Square. A City Council Highways examination confirmed that high voltage electricity cables were present but deep enough underground to have no effect on the statue. Contractors Rosgal, working in association with their suppliers O'Connors arrived on site to install the reinforced concrete base into which the statue would be embedded.

▼ *The statue base showing the exposed high voltage cable; 30th October 2018*

▲ *Meeting circle under construction; 11th July 2018*

On 9th July 2018, a seminal moment arrived for the statue campaign. The installation of the meeting circle began. Over the next four days Jeremy and his team positioned the stones, installed the skateboard inhibitors and completed the carving of the words:

'Deeds not words, Rise Up Women, Emmeline Pankhurst 1858 - 1928, Hazel Reeves'.

▼ *'Deeds not Words' being carved;11th July 2018*

The entrance to the meeting circle was carefully planned to face the former Free Trade Hall, given its significance in suffragette history.

The meeting circle was unveiled on Sunday 15th July 2018; Emmeline Pankhurst's 160th birthday. I opened proceedings as Chair of the Campaign, Rosie Garland led a community singing of 'March of the Women' and 'Happy Birthday'. The Lord Mayor of Manchester, Councillor June Hitchen, welcomed everybody, whilst Dr Helen Pankhurst outlined the significance of the event. Hazel Reeves hailed the meeting circle as an important moment in the statue process.

The BBC cameraman on the day discovered the parabolic sound mirror effect of the stonework; stand in the middle of the circle and hear your words echoing back at you.

On 25th October 2018, I headed for East London and the Bronze Age foundry occupying arches under the Docklands Light Railway. Hazel has worked with Bronze Age on all her major projects including Sir Nigel Gresley and The Cracker Packers. Their role would be to turn Hazel's wax creation into bronze using the 'lost wax' process.

The bronze itself is heated to 1,175 degrees Centigrade and then poured into the ceramic shell created around the wax model. To facilitate the process the statue is broken into a number of pieces.

▲ *The bronze being poured at Bronze Age; 25th October 2018*

▲ *The Lord Mayor, Councillor June Hitchen, Hazel, Helen and Andrew at the unveiling of the meeting circle; 15th July 2018*

In the run up to the unveiling of the statue all manner of preparations were made; the staging and management was organised with the City Council's events team for the ceremony in St Peter's Square, meetings with Metrolink, agreeing the route and timetables for the two marches, finding enough event space to host the seven hundred guests, sending out invitations, inviting schools to participate, ordering six thousand ponchos to hand out to participants in case of wet weather.

On 22nd November 2018, I held an excellent meeting with Aline Frantzen, Managing Director of Metrolink. Although the trams wouldn't stop running on the day, they would be paused at the critical points during the event, the tram wheels would be oiled to reduce noise and they wouldn't sound their horns as they passed through St Peter's Square. Metrolink themselves would provide additional security and would publicise the unveiling in the run up to the day.

▲ *Bridget Aherne and Aline Frantzen of Metrolink with the maquette: 22nd November 2018*

Sculptor Hazel Reeves and Emmeline's great great grandaughter, Helen Pankhurst, share a moment with Emmeline at the end of the unveiling ceremony. ▶

On Thursday 13th December 2018 the Emmeline Pankhurst statue arrived in St Peter's Square.

On Friday 14th December 2018, 'Our Emmeline' was unveiled in front of a huge crowd in St. Peter's Square. The photographers and cameramen jostled for the best position in front of the statue. After speeches from myself and others, including Helen Pankhurst, Fatima Shahid, Sarah Judge and Baroness Williams, Emmeline was revealed in all her glory to tumultuous applause. Hazel Reeves gave the final speech.

All the hard work had finally paid off.

▲ *Manchester Community Choir, directed by Liz Power,
sing a heartfelt rendition of 'Nana Was a Suffragette'.*

*Crowds stand with their arms
outstretched, copying Emmeline -
a fitting tribute for the occasion.* ▶

Marchers arriving in St. Peter's Square, chanting and channelling the suffragettes. ▲

'It is an added pleasure to me that you are a woman.'

There is a letter within the Annie Horniman papers at the University of Manchester that bears the signature of Emmeline Pankhurst, the leader of the Women's Social and Political Union (WSPU). She wrote to Annie in congratulations on receiving her honorary degree from the University of Manchester:

'…you have done so much for dramatic art in this country that you have won our gratitude. It is added pleasure to me that you are a woman.'

Annie had been a key player in revolutionising the theatre movement, a movement which, through the Actresses' Franchise League, advocated and campaigned for the vote alongside the WSPU. Like Emmeline, she too was a considered an unorthodox character, acting outside of the boundaries of what was expected of middle-class, respectable women. It is undoubtedly what the four women in this section, though separated by centuries, have in common. Although they all came from positions of privilege, the legacy they left behind in the city inspired new and bold artistic and creative conceptions by women from all walks of life and all cultures, to be revered and celebrated not only in Manchester but internationally.

Elizabeth Gaskell, Enriqueta Rylands, Annie Horniman and Olive Shapley shaped the cultural scene of Manchester in their own right. Each had their own unique method - supporting new playwrights, writing novels exposing the real lives of working women, opening public spaces to encourage learning and creating documentaries that, for one of the first times, gave working men and women a public voice. Manchester and its surroundings was undoubtedly their muse, its landscape and its people the perfect inspiration for their art.

Women had to fight to be accepted into this world, but once there, they were there to stay. Manchester's rich cultural heritage did not start and end with North and South, or Annie Horniman's Gaiety Theatre. Today, Manchester is recognised internationally for its music, art and theatre - from the Bridgewater Hall to Manchester Art Gallery. Amongst these famous spots, still standing are the historic homes and places inhabited by the women representing the arts on this long-list. John Rylands Library, built by **Enriqueta Rylands**, opens its doors to thousands of visitors a year. At Plymouth Grove, tourists and visitors can pay pilgrimage to the family home of **Elizabeth Gaskell**, the author of novels *Mary Barton* and *North and South*.

Although the house at Plymouth Grove represents the comfortable and cultural lifestyle of the Gaskell family, her novels held up a mirror to the lives of those in Manchester and the brutal realities of industrial life. Elizabeth's novels were not published under a male pseudonym and her work appealed to female readers, intrigued by the heroines she created and their reflection of realistic and often tragic domestic spheres. Her role as the female author, alongside the Brontë sisters, would have encouraged other women to write. Indeed, in a letter to an unknown acquaintance who had enclosed work for her to read, she responds by explaining the struggle of balancing the upkeep of her domestic role with her writing:

'...a good writer of fiction must have lived an active and sympathetic life if she wishes her books to have strength and vitality in them. When you are forty, and if you have the gift of being an authoress, you will write ten times the novel as you could do now, just because you will have gone through so much more of the interests of a wife and a mother.'

Through the end of the 19th and the beginning of the 20th century, women such as Lydia Becker formed societies for women to discuss books and scientific endeavours. As the domestic spheres of middle-class women became distorted, more women took a direct interest in politics, art and literature. When the Pankhurst Memorial Hall first opened in 1900, it offered lectures in science and arts, and the Free Trade Hall, funded by the Anti-Corn Law League and built on the site of the Peterloo massacre, was another place for educational advancement. Women were welcomed into Manchester Art Gallery and Manchester Museum. Manchester Museum, which had opened its doors in 1888, employed some of the first female curatorial staff. In 1910, Grace Wigglesworth was made Assistant Keeper of Botany after studying at Owen's College, whilst Winifred Crompton was the Assistant Keeper of Egyptology. Women were not only beginning to access culture but were becoming qualified to provide it.

Access to museums and galleries, the John Ryland's Library, the Portico Library and the theatres of the city, increased cultural awareness even further. Alice Foley, a young socialist and the first female secretary of the Weavers' Association, wrote of the importance of these trips when she was a young working-class woman in her autobiography, A *Bolton Childhood*:

'...I hoarded my scanty pocket-money, amounting at that time to one penny in the shilling of factory earnings, so that I could afford with them the luxury of a monthly matinee. With a cheap seat in pit or a gallery we saw most of the early Shaw and Galsworthy plays, followed by tea in the Clarion Café in Market Street... If the café was crowded, we hived off to the Art Gallery and over tea, brown bread, peaches and cream, we animatedly argued and discussed the philosophy, art or satire of the productions. The whole outing cost about five shillings about, but we returned home like exultant gods...'

Where **Olive Shapley** began her work sharing the stories of everyday northern lives, the legacy of her work lives on in Media City, now at Salford Quays. Indeed, BBC Radio Manchester helped mark the centenary in the city and ran a competition called *Manchester Monologues*, encouraging people to write three-minute monologues that were not necessarily written by women in Manchester, but were inspired by the past and present women of Manchester. Although it was judged anonymously, all five winners were women from Greater Manchester. Their work was performed by actors at *Suffragette City*, a centenary celebration event held at the Royal Exchange Theatre.

Thinking has many a time made me sad darling; but doing never did in all my life... My precept is do something my sister; if you can do good, but at any rate do something.

ELIZABETH GASKELL

In North and South, a tale of love, industry and smoke, our heroine Margaret Hale moves to the mill town of Milton, a place almost identical to the heavily industrialised Manchester. Her first encounter with the place is less than positive:

'Nearer the town, the air had a faint taste and smell of smoke; perhaps, after all, more a loss of the fragrance of grass and herbage than any positive taste or smell. Quick they were whirled over long, straight, hopeless streets of regularly-built houses, all small and of brick. Here and there among her chickens, puffing out black "unparliamentary" smoke, and sufficiently accounting for the cloud which Margaret had taken to foretell rain.'

Margaret had never seen an industrial city before, explaining her faux pas at thinking the smoke-filled sky was rain (although if Milton is Manchester, this would not have been a far-off guess either). Her initial horror of the place softens a little over the course of the novel, helped perhaps by her relationship with mill owner John Thornton and her close friendship with the Higgins family, weavers and union members. But Manchester – or Milton – is merely the foundation of a story of personal growth, challenging social normalities, hierarchy, prejudices and, perhaps above all, defying authority to do what is right. Margaret Hale, young though she may be, takes the burdens of her family and the struggles of others on her shoulders. She emerges at the end of the novel in control of her life, her finances and her romantic liaisons.

The creator of Margaret Hale was Elizabeth Gaskell. Equally strong-minded, philanthropic and intelligent, Elizabeth became one of the most recognised authors of the mid-Victorian age. Like her fellow writers and eventual acquaintances, Charles Dickens and Charlotte Brontë, Elizabeth wrote about the realities of life, of romance, of poverty, painting a sometimes bleak and haunting picture of life in Manchester.

Illustration by **Artsynibs**

As Friedrich Engels carried out his damning assessment of the slums of the city, Elizabeth explored the lives of those she walked past every day, writing in the foreword of Mary Barton:

'I had always felt a deep sympathy with the care-worn men, who looked as if doomed to struggle through their lives in strange alternations between work and want; tossed to and fro by circumstances, apparently in even a greater degree than other men. A little manifestation of this sympathy, and a little attention to the expression of feelings on the part of some of the work-people with whom I was acquainted, had laid open to me the hearts of one or two of the more thoughtful among them...'

Elizabeth was, like her famous novel, a mixture of north and south. She was born in London in 1810. Like Mr Hale in *North and South*, her father had been a minister in the church but had left due to intellectual differences. When her mother died nearly a year after she was born, Elizabeth was sent to Cheshire, where she was to be raised by her aunt, who she often said was more like a mother to her. Brought up in Knutsford, Elizabeth was raised strongly in the Unitarian faith, something that would impact both her professional and personal life immensely over the years. Her upbringing around Cheshire often brought her into proximity with the city that would later dominate her writing. She had a strong education, both at home from her aunt and at the Unitarian school she attended until she was fifteen. Growing up, she travelled between relatives, including her somewhat estranged father and stepmother, to various aunts around the country. Like her fellow author and future friend Charlotte Bronte, Elizabeth spent time in Europe during her youth.

Although early writings of Elizabeth's are not recorded, her letters and her biographers surmise she had always held the talent of the pen.

When examining her work and her portrait of the industrial town and its people, it is clear Elizabeth's faith had a massive impact on how she portrayed her characters. Elizabeth drew from her own personal experiences, as well as the political climate and the people that she brushed elbows with on the street. In *Mary Barton, North and South*, and *Ruth*, Elizabeth created characters with strength, empathy and resilience, who were not creators of their misfortune, but often the result of the economic climate of the day.

Elizabeth began writing what we might call seriously whilst in mourning for her son. She had married William Gaskell, a Unitarian minister, in 1832. Four of Elizabeth's six children survived infancy; but it was at her lowest ebb, mourning her dead child, that writing brought her strength and solace. The result, *Mary Barton*, was sold and published anonymously, although soon enough, Elizabeth's identity, 'Mrs Gaskell', was revealed.

Elizabeth's debut novel was heralded by the literary giants of the day. Charles Dickens began to publish her short stories and serialised works in his journal, *Household Words*. Dickens would continue to champion her work, saying: 'There is no living English writer whose aid I would desire to enlist in preference to the authoress of *Mary Barton* (a book that most profoundly affected and impressed me)'. Dickens would remain a staunch supporter of her work, though he lamented her tendency to miss deadlines for the journal.

As she grew to become a household name, Elizabeth shared correspondence, and often close friendships, with fellow female authors, perhaps most famously Charlotte Brontë, author of *Jane Eyre* and *Villette*. *Jane Eyre* had been published the year before Mary Barton, under the pseudonym Currer Bell, alongside the works of Acton and Ellis – Charlotte's sisters, Anne and Emily. Charlotte's life had been marred by the loss of her siblings to tuberculosis within a matter of months and although her relationship with Elizabeth would never replace that which she had with her sisters, they shared an altogether cordial friendship. Elizabeth visited Charlotte at the parsonage in Haworth where she lived with her father; the visit was later reciprocated. The strength of their friendship is perhaps shown through Elizabeth's biography of Charlotte, written after her death and littered with scenes of her early life and conversations with her father that Charlotte must have shared with her.

Interestingly, it is in a letter she writes to Dickens that Elizabeth's commitment to the support of young woman is evident. Writing about poverty was a bit like putting your money where your mouth is and Elizabeth did not shy away from it, as her faith and morals directed her to, and she gave generously to charitable organisations. In a letter from January 1850, Elizabeth wrote to Dickens, imploring for his help with a charitable case: 'I want some help, and I cannot think of anybody who can give it to me so well as you...' Elizabeth continues to write of a young woman imprisoned at the New Bailey, who had been orphaned and had fallen on hard times. Elizabeth had been to visit her and needed Dickens' financial assistance in bringing the girl into a Miss Coutts refuge for reformed female prisoners. Her dedication to helping young women and giving charitably to these causes is a testament to her determined and generous character.

Elizabeth's writing made her well-known to the public and indeed, sent many literary celebrities and cultural names to visit her in Manchester. However, the impact of Elizabeth and William Gaskell upon Manchester stretches far beyond the realms of her literary work. Whilst Mrs Gaskell was by no means the person who put Manchester on the map, many of the places in the city that furthered academic thinking, philosophical teachings and earned Manchester the reputation of a forward-thinking, liberal city, were supported and patronised by William and Elizabeth. The Portico Library and the Manchester Literary and Philosophical Association were both patronised by the Gaskells. In 1859, Elizabeth wrote to George Eliot, alias of Mary Ann Evans, author of Middlemarch:

'I…went plodging through our Manchester Sts to get every number [of Eliot's Scenes of Clerical Life] as soon as it was accessible from the Portico reading table.'

Cross Street Chapel was destroyed in the Second World War, but it stands, rebuilt, in the same place today. William Gaskell began his career as Assistant Minister there and rose to Senior Minister, where he spent over fifty years of his life. It remains today a place for theological debate and conversation. Then, Members of Parliament, scholars, merchants and the middle classes would have sat in the congregation, alongside the working-class men and women of the city. It was a place dedicated to social and educational change; four of the scholars who set up the progressive Owen's College in Manchester – where William would later teach – were congregants at Cross Street Chapel. William and Elizabeth were especially committed to education for all. Over the course of their time in Manchester, they would provide aid, finance and relief, particularly during harsh times like the Cotton Famine.

In 1850, along with her husband and her daughters, Elizabeth Gaskell moved to a 84 Plymouth Grove, a house that still stands today. A stone's throw away from where the Pankhurst family would later reside, back then the house was surrounded by fresh air and fields. Elizabeth wrote to her friend, Eliza Fox, of its purchase:

"We've got a house…it certainly is a beauty…I must try and make the house give as much pleasure to others as I can."

The house at Plymouth Grove seemed to become an extension of all the places they visited, spoke of and supported in Manchester. Unlike her friend Charlotte Brontë, Elizabeth adored visitors and busy crowds. The rooms at Plymouth Grove soon began to swell with social endeavours and excellent conversation. As well as Charlotte Brontë, Elizabeth Gaskell had social calls and visits from some of the most celebrated names in Victorian cultural society; John Ruskin and Charles Halle were both friendly with the Gaskells. Elizabeth's four daughters, Marianne, Margaret, Florence and Julia, were accomplished young women who joined their parents in entertaining the many guests at the house.

Elizabeth died in 1865, at the house in Hampshire she had planned to buy as a surprise for her family. William, with two of their daughters, remained at Plymouth Grove and continued to run the hub of lively conversation, debate, music and discussion, until 1913, when the last Gaskell passed away.

The house became a shadow of its former self, until it was restored by the Manchester Historic Buildings Trust and a £2 million grant from the Heritage Lottery Fund; it opened to the public in 2014. The house has been recreated using descriptions of how it would have looked when the Gaskell family inhabited the house.

Elizabeth's life was full of energy, of resolve and was led by her social responsibility to document and attempt to ease the suffering she saw in Manchester. Whilst she is remembered today as one of the most prolific writers of the 19th Century, her legacy as a champion of intellectual debate and charitable work continues within the walls of 84 Plymouth Grove and in the novels that sit on the shelves of libraries, homes and classrooms today.

ENRIQUETA RYLANDS

As we will come to discover throughout this book, chasing the lives of great and radical women is made immensely difficult by the lack of paper trails they leave behind. Whether their personal correspondence was destroyed at their bequest, on the orders of concerned family members, or simply whether they were too poor or insignificant to be kept, without letters or journals, it is impossible to know the real person behind what could be seen as a public façade.

Enriqueta Rylands is one of these enigmatic women. Lost in a sea of revolutionary women who inhabited the city at the time and who were shouting louder about their dedicated causes, Enriqueta is easily overlooked. One of the wealthiest women of her day, Enriqueta was the founder of John Rylands Library, a cultural gem that since it opened more than a hundred years ago, has been a landmark for literary lovers and historians from around the world. Enriqueta commissioned the library as a memorial to her husband but used her architectural and literary intellect to design and fill it. The library was a public venture – it was made for the people of Manchester, a parting gift from one of the biggest philanthropists of the day, and a sign that his wife would continue this legacy after his death.

Enriqueta did not have the usual upbringing one would expect of the widow of a wealthy man. She did not begin her life in her adopted city of Manchester, but was born on 31st May 1843, as far away from the city as was imaginable at the time – in Havana, Cuba. Enriqueta was one of five siblings born to Stephen Cattley Tennant and his wife, Spanish-born Juana Camila Dalcour. Stephen was a merchant for a firm in Liverpool, with some

sources noting him as a sugar planter. The family returned to Liverpool in 1848 when Enriqueta was five years old. Despite her father's intention to retire, he died tragically in the same year after falling off the train platform at Farnborough station and becoming trapped beneath it.

Her mother relocated the family to Paris, where she remarried the composer, pianist and close friend of Chopin, Julian Fontana. Fontana had played in Havana in 1844, where he had met Camila, who at the time was twenty-six years old, married, with children. Whether a romantic attachment or merely a friendly one was made, we do not know. The marriage produced a son and Camila was pregnant with their second child when, in 1855, she died suddenly after a short illness. At twelve years old, Enriqueta had become an orphan. It was a long time before she would know security and stability again.

Little is known about the life Enriqueta led before eventually arriving in Manchester. With the home of her father's relations in Liverpool acting as a base, she carried out her education at a convent school in New York. It's impossible to know what her thoughts were on what must have been a tiring journey across the sea, to such an expanding, wealthy city; was she alone with a chaperone? Did her siblings travel with her? Was it here that her love of literature and knowledge was fueled and stirred? We may never know. After completing her final years of school in Paris, Enriqueta returned to Liverpool.

The paper trail of Enriqueta's life does not re-emerge until the 1860s. What we can decipher perhaps, from her life of travelling

Illustration by **Helen Musselwhite**

87

and movement, her upbringing around merchants in Liverpool and artists and musicians in Paris, is that Enriqueta lived a life of some excitement, steeped in education and appreciation for culture.

Whilst women across Britain were establishing themselves as intellectual leaders of literature, arts and sciences, there were still limits as to what women could study, as opposed to men. Within Enriqueta's lifetime, women were able to study at institutions of high education but were not allowed to graduate with a degree. Aside from these few women – the first who took their examinations in 1849 – the education of upper and middle-class women would have been a basic grasp of literature, music and languages - tools that would aid them in society and marriage. For working-class women, further education was almost entirely unachievable.

Although, to our knowledge, she was not educated beyond what was expected of women at the time, by the time she had joined John Rylands' household in the early 1860s, she was described by their minister, Joseph Parker, as: '...young, vivacious and accomplished.'

Enriqueta was employed at roughly the age of twenty by John Rylands' wife, Martha, to be her companion. John Rylands, a giant in the textile industry who had vast shares in the Manchester Ship Canal, was the first multi-millionaire of the city, having amassed an incredible fortune through investment in the city's industry. The family lived in Longford Hall near Stretford and amidst their own grief of losing their eldest son, the Rylands must have welcomed Enriqueta's energy and vitality into their home.

Sometime after the death of Martha Rylands in 1875, Enriqueta and John were married. Although more than forty years John's junior, Enriqueta must have made an engaging and uplifting companion for a man who had suffered so much personal loss. During their marriage, Enriqueta took a keen interest in the generosity of her husband, investing her time into the charities he patronised. The Rylands, like many others, were led by their strong Christian faith and believed this could guide others. They supported several chapels across the city, as well as donating to orphanages, schools and charities for the poor. John and Enriqueta, both at this stage childless, adopted two children, Arthur and Maria. Their life together was contented and as John approached frailty, Enriqueta nursed him through his old age.

John died in 1888 at the age of 87 and Enriqueta, suddenly left an overwhelmingly vast fortune, was named executor of his will. For the first time ever, the shroud of mystery surrounding her life was suddenly lifted. Enriqueta had to step into the shoes of the wealthiest philanthropist Manchester had ever known. Surrounded by trusted advisors, Enriqueta continued to ensure the legacy of Rylands and Sons, as well as retaining the shares in the Manchester Ship Canal, which had saved the project from collapse. Having spent much of her life as a companion, wife and daughter, Enriqueta was now applying her robust education and charismatic personality to this new role. One project, however, would soon demonstrate Enriqueta's strength, determination and ability to deliver.

The idea of a public memorial to John Rylands after his death would not have been a preposterous or far-fetched one; after all, he had done so much for Manchester throughout his life, from funding the Manchester Ship Canal to his many charitable ventures. Enriqueta could have commissioned a statue, or a stone memorial, or even another Congregationalist chapel in his name. Instead, she settled on a public space for the people of Manchester – a vast and ornate library, that would rival the esteemed colleges of Oxford. Manchester was known for its business ventures, not its books, but Rylands had been dedicated to bible and theological study. To Enriqueta, a place of similar learning and teaching seemed the perfect way to memorialise him.

What became clear was who owned this project; it was not the company's trustees, the architects or the builders, it was Enriqueta. She invested over £1million of her money into the library, and absolutely insisted on being consulted at every stage. This was a woman who had travelled across the world and who had sight and knowledge of how cultural establishments should look and feel.

The library took over ten years to complete. Enriqueta had commissioned architect Basil Champneys, who had been responsible for the design of many of the Oxford colleges that Enriqueta admired, including Mansfield. Champneys and Enriqueta were known to clash over the details of the building and Enriqueta demanded the final say over everything.

The location of the library was carefully chosen. Deansgate had always been divided by class throughout the 19th Century, housing some of the worst slums and crime districts throughout Manchester. It was here that charities such as the Wood Street Mission carried out their work, trying to support and care for those who lived there. Enriqueta herself was a known benefactor of the Mission, requesting that one of her donations went towards 'an old woman's heat.' It seems fitting, considering both Enriqueta and John Rylands' charitable generosity, that the site of their library would be where one of the worst slums of Manchester had recently been cleared, symbolising a cultural renaissance for the city.

Enriqueta took charge of the library's contents just as determinedly as she had overseen the designs for the building. In 1892, Enriqueta made a milestone purchase for the library when she bought the entirety of the Althorp Library collection from the 5th Earl Spencer, for a record sum of £210,000. Subsequently, forty thousand volumes, many rare and precious, made their way into the collection, becoming the foundation on which the rest of the library would be built.

In building this sensational new collection of precious works, Enriqueta understood the need for it to be catalogued. She appointed a head librarian, but also employed Alice Cooke to catalogue and index the Althorp Library collection. Alice, like many of the women on the periphery of cultural and political life in Manchester, could herself have been considered a candidate for the statue long-list. Alice was the first woman to achieve an MA degree from Owen's College in Manchester and went on to become the first female lecturer at the college. Alice catalogued the Althorp collection that sat at the heart of the library, as Enriqueta continued to collect and purchase new additions for the library, often, as she had done with the Althorp collection, anonymously.

On 6th October 1899, what would have been John and Enriqueta's anniversary, John Rylands Library was officially inaugurated. Enriqueta was presented with the Freedom of the City, the first woman in Manchester to be given this honour. The library opened to the public on 1st January 1890.

There is something rather poignant, perhaps ironic, about who we think about when walking past the library. It bears John Rylands' name – the name of the greatest textile merchant, public benefactor and Manchester's first multi-millionaire. However, it is undoubtedly the legacy of one woman, a woman who invested so much into the literature and culture of Manchester. Enriqueta's name does not sit within the public memory of Manchester, despite all she achieved. Despite her statue within the library, it is perhaps time that Enriqueta's name overshadows that of her husband and we remember the incredible jewel in Manchester's crown as her legacy and not his.

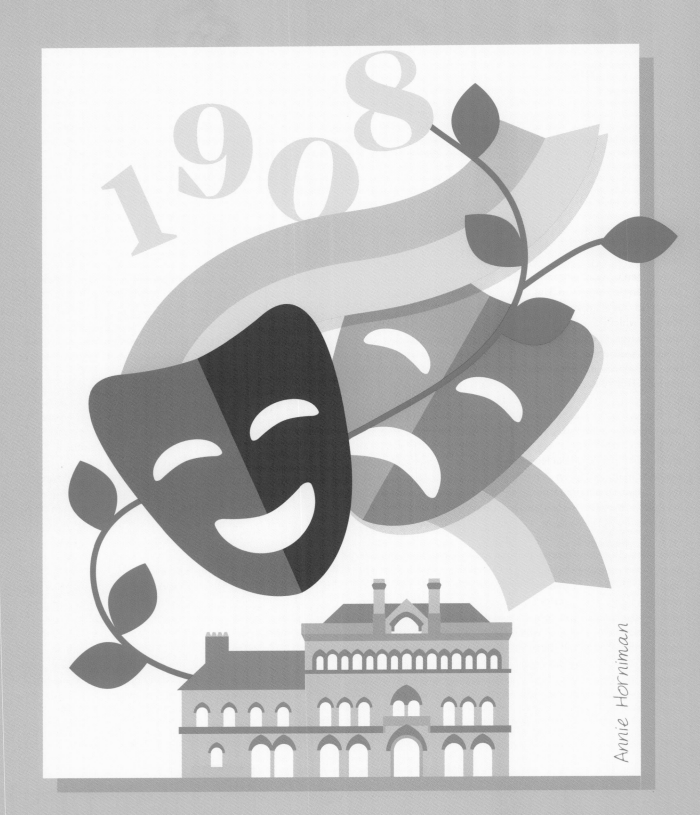

ANNIE HORNIMAN

There aren't many women, past or present, who have led a life like Annie Horniman. Her name has survived as part of the great Horniman dynasty and lends itself to the museum in London, which Annie helped to establish. A pioneer of theatre, Annie's whole life seems like a production – something staged, magical and fascinating to watch unfold. From suffrage to the occult, Annie's interests were wide-ranging and often controversial, but she stared opposition in the face and cared little about what people thought of her. Although not originally from Manchester, the city owes her a great debt for bringing a new wave of literary talent and culture to its streets.

Annie Elizabeth Fredricka Horniman was born into a successful tea merchant family on 3rd October 1860, to Rebekah and Fredrick Horniman. Her father took over his father's tea business in 1868 and travelled across the world, both for pleasure and with the Horniman Tea Company. The family lived at Surrey Mount in considerable comfort, living, essentially in a micro-version of the British Museum. Fredrick Horniman's fascination with world history and ethnography led him to acquire a vast collection of objects and artefacts that he eventually turned into the Surrey World Museum. On Fredrick's death in 1906, Annie's childhood home was gifted to the council, eventually paving the way for the Horniman Museum, of which Fredrick's massive collection became the foundation. Both Annie's father and brother were liberal MPs, but Annie did not share their zeal for the political sphere, despite her support of the women's suffrage movement, and instead turned her hand to the arts.

Annie and her brother were rather sheltered throughout their childhood, adhering to their parents' strict, religious household. They were educated at home, never attending school, and it was not until the age of fourteen that Annie saw her first play, William Shakespeare's The Merchant of Venice, when her governess secreted her and her brother Elmslie to the theatre. From then on, Annie's creative passions were ignited and from putting on secret performances with her brother, Annie would go on to produce and fund progressive and powerful pieces of theatre, created by some of the most notable playwrights of the century. First, she had to get out from under the wing of her father and his beliefs that the theatre was sinful. In 1882, Annie joined the Slade School of Art despite having little artistic talent and spent four years there, unleashing a vivacious and powerful personality that her strict upbringing had repressed. Her relationship with her father ultimately ended when her mother died and he remarried a young woman forty years his junior. Annie, disapproving of the match, cut off all contact.

Annie dressed lavishly, smoked heavily and shingled her long hair, embracing modern styles and changes. She moved in fascinating circles and the school now gave her the freedom to explore her love of theatre and the arts. Now of age and with her own independent means, Annie took up her father's passion for travelling and moved through Europe on her bicycle. The bicycle had liberated women, offering new experiences and the chance of solo transport. Despite many opponents believing them to offer a 'sexual awakening' for women due to the design of the frame, women began to shed their restrictive skirts for 'bicycle bloomers'. Annie hated the design of bicycles made specifically for women, preferring the more robust male frames.

Illustration by **Amy Rodchester**

91

On her return to the UK – wealthy, independent, and with a growing reputation for eccentricity – Annie was introduced to a new, fashionable and mysterious religion: spiritualism and the occult. Through her friendship with Mina Bergson from the Slade School of Art, Annie was introduced to the mystical and spiritual Hermetic Order of the Golden Dawn, where she developed the relationships and beliefs that would shape her future, both in and outside of the theatre. Other members included noted playwrights, artists and creatives such as the actress Florence Farr, whom Annie went on to anonymously finance a season of plays for. The season included a play by Yeats and the first public performance of a play by George Bernard Shaw. Although critically acclaimed, it was a financial failure. Annie funded many of the artists, including Mina and her husband Samuel Liddell MacGregor Mathers, one of the founders of the Order of the Golden Dawn. Annie was a powerful and high-ranking member of the Order for thirteen years, until a disagreement over the practice of sex in rituals – something she disagreed with strongly – led to her expulsion.

Annie met William Butler Yeats in 1903, through their shared interest in the occult. Fascinated by his work, Annie patronised him and worked by his side, unpaid, assisting him with his publications, often as his scribe. Their relationship was intense, and long-lasting; some have questioned Annie's devotion to Yeats and whether it was truly reciprocated, as Yeats knew he could get money from Annie to support his theatrical ventures. But Annie had always recognised true talent and her devotion to the arts carried their creative partnership for years.

In 1904, Annie found a home for the Irish National Playwright Society, when she funded the transformation of the old Mechanics Institute in Dublin into the historic Abbey Theatre. Here, playwrights like Yeats and Augusta Gregory began to put on progressive pieces of theatre. Some members of the theatre found Annie over-bearing, for she wanted a say in all activity that happened and many scholars have referred to her simply as an interfering spinster who Yeats had tapped for gold. However, this was the world that Annie knew and loved.

Now that she could finally and openly patronise the arts, she would never have taken a step back and watched it play out in front of her. Annie, as ever, was the main player.

Her work in Ireland sadly came to an end in 1910. The political tensions around nationalism and Home Rule proved too much for Annie to comprehend. When the theatre remained open the day after the King's death, when all others had closed out of respect, Annie withdrew her support – and her money – from the venture.

But this would not be Annie's last foray into the theatre. In Manchester, Annie flourished again. In 1908, two years before she pulled out of the Abbey Theatre, Annie purchased The Gaiety Theatre on Peter Street. The Gaiety Theatre had been built in 1884 and served as a comedy theatre, run by the United Theatre Company. Annie hired Ben Payne, an actor and theatre manager, to manage the theatre and to acquire premises and actors. According to Payne, Yeats advised him to make his contract 'tight...laying down limits beyond which Miss Horniman had no authority or right to interfere.' He later wrote to local newspapers to announce Annie's desire to form a repertory theatre, emphasising the commitment to 'serious works of art' and:

'…an especially widely open door to present day British writers, who will not now need to sigh in vain for a hearing, provided only that they have something to say worth listening to, and say it in an interesting and original manner.'

Manchester, Annie believed, was ready for its first repertory theatre. The city matched all of Annie's needs: it was cheap in comparison to London, it was socially and politically progressive (the women's suffrage movement was in full swing at this stage) and it had a growing cultural movement. Annie and her company remodelled the entire theatre after one season run, updating the run-down interior with comfortable seating, arranged so that everybody in the audience could see and hear the performance adequately. The programmes were adorned with symbols of spiritualism, including the six-pointed pentagon.

The theatre thrived at first. The stage was offered to playwrights who fitted Annie's bill: serious, profound and progressive. The Manchester School of Dramatists were formed from the work produced at the Gaiety and from playwrights such as George Bernard Shaw, Stanley Houghton, Harold Brighouse and Allan Monkhouse. Annie became a well-known sight in Manchester, holding court at the Midland Hotel. Payne described her at an early meeting with the Manchester Playgoers' Club:

'She was dressed, as was her custom on formal occasions, in a richer than usual costume of original design suggestive, as I have said, of medieval attire… its material was gold brocade, and she wore – I saw it for the first time – her famous opal-studded dragon, at least five inches across, which hung like an insignia on her bosom.'

In 1910, Annie was awarded an honorary degree from the University of Manchester for her services to the theatrical arts and Annie proudly wore her robes, often combined with her elaborate and decorative jewellery (her opal-studded dragon, in particular), on several occasions. For almost a decade, the Gaiety entertained the working people of Manchester, but the combination of the First World War and the heavy, often gloomy tone of the plays produced, meant that Annie's vision of the Gaiety Theatre came to an end in 1917. It was leased to travelling theatre companies before Annie sold it in 1921, retiring permanently back to London.

For her services to theatre and her role in bringing the Repertory Movement to life, Annie was made a Companion of Honour in 1933. Before her death, she continued to travel and hold court with her wide circle of friends and companions, as eccentric and extravagant as ever. She died on 6th August 1937, in her sleep.

Complaints were made about Annie throughout her life – of her interference, of her stubbornness and her flamboyance. Yeats, despite their fondness for each other, denounced her as a 'vulgarian'. Yet Annie was a woman who carved her own path at a time when women, whether through politics, through arts, or, as she found, through theatre, were becoming confident at talking back, standing up for themselves and fulfilling the roles that they had only dreamed of before. Her inspiration was far-reaching; in a later biography, Lilian Baylis, one of the key figures in the running of the Old Vic, summarised Annie's influence neatly:

'Lilian Baylis has stated that it was the influence of Miss Horniman that led her to starting the Old Vic. What woman could do, she thought, another could do.'

OLIVE SHAPLEY

When announcing the engagement of John Salt, a BBC executive, in 1939, the Daily Mail claimed that he would wed a girl: '...whose voice was known to millions.' They were not wrong. During the inter-war period, Olive Shapley was one of the most well-known radical voices on the airwaves. Having made her home in Manchester, away from her native Peckham, Olive produced hard-hitting and brutally eye-opening documentaries about real people and their lives, their jobs and their opinions. Despite facing internal conservatism and, as many working women at the time did, workplace sexism, Olive pioneered. From presenting Woman's Hour to creating a safe house for abused women, Olive's remained a voice not only known to millions of people, but as the voice who spoke out for them.

Olive was born on 10th April 1910, in Peckham, London. Her parents, William and Kate, met at a Unitarian church and were married soon after. Olive was the youngest child, having two elder brothers. Her oldest brother, Frank, died in the First World War at the Battle of Jutland, having lied about his age in order to join the navy. He had been spurred on by a woman handing him a white feather (indicating cowardice for not signing up) whilst he was on a trip with his scout troop. To suffer such personal tragedy at such a young age was tragically not uncommon during the war and Olive suffered nightmares and distress for years after.

William worked for London County Council as a sanitation inspector and would often take Olive on visits with him. It was during these visits that she encountered all walks of life, from working-class families to the Chinese communities in East London. Her family, Olive claimed in her autobiography, bore none of the xenophobia that others had at the time. The family were relatively liberal – her mother's brothers were both socialists, although her father 'thought Labour and voted Conservative.' There were lively political debates in the Shapley household and Olive's political interests were broadened further when she was sent on a trip to stay with the aunt of a schoolfriend. 'Aunt Annie', a headmistress, had been a suffragette, a word that Olive didn't understand at first. She 'had an absolute conviction that she knew best.' It was Olive's first exposure to a woman with such strong principles, and once she understood what a suffragette was, the crocheted green and purple egg cosies made more sense.

Olive attended Mary Datchelor Girls' School, where she excelled and developed a passion for history. It was during her time here, at the party of a schoolfriend, that Olive first listened to the wireless – a contraption she had never heard of before. The scratchy overtones and faraway voice was, to her, 'impressive... but not overly so.' This moment didn't inspire her future career and when she gained a place at Oxford, she planned on either becoming a Unitarian minister or a history teacher.

Illustration by **Nicola Fernandes**

Olive had a place at St Hugh's College, which was, at the time, a women's-only college. She had some notable friends and fellow students here, including Barbara Castle, who, Olive said of their first meeting, '...*spent most of the time telling me how infinitely superior the north was to the south.*' Barbara went on to become a Labour MP and life peer and was instrumental in the Equal Pay Act (1970). It was during the summer months, on a visit to Barbara's family in Hyde, that Olive fell in love with the north-west and vowed to return.

It was as a young student at Oxford that Olive had a brief entanglement with communism. As political tensions mounted across Europe and fascist Germany grew in power, it is no surprise that Olive saw communism as a method of resistance. She was a founding member of the October Club, a place for communist students to debate and discuss the works of Marx and Engels. The group even hosted the Jarrow Marchers as they came through Oxford, horrified at their living and working conditions. Although she was a member of the Communist Party, Olive never signed up fully as she would have been dismissed from Oxford if discovered. Later in life, despite losing interest in radical politics, Olive had a political blot on her file because of these communist activities.

Olive trained to be a teacher and went on to lecture for the Worker's Education Association before training as a nursery teacher. Before she finished her qualification, however, an advertisement had caught her mother's eye. In 1934, Olive applied for the position of *Children's Hour* Organiser at the BBC. Her first reaction to the mere notion of applying?

The British Broadcasting Corporation (BBC) had launched in 1922 with a single programme and had grown over the years to become one of the most significant and influential establishments in the country. The stereotypical picture of the BBC at this time was a male-dominated and perhaps London-centric one. This, however, is skewed. The BBC employed hundreds of women; many were employed as cleaners, or clerical and secretarial staff, whilst some were involved in the research and production of programmes and broadcasts. Women such as Elise Sprott joined the BBC in 1924 and publicly challenged the 'silent women' who worked in the background to produce these programmes.

Sure enough, more and more female voices began to sound out over the airwaves. Regional news and programming were also important and Manchester was the home of BBC North, one of the four regional transmission stations. It was into this world of northern programming that Olive stepped in 1934. Although her career was launched at *Children's Hour*, she disliked the show. This was the place where most women were employed, for the natural assumption that a woman should produce maternal, comforting shows for children remained in place. Olive would oversee the production of two plays a week, soundtracked by the BBC North Orchestra. One of the first instructions she received here, whilst finding her feet in a hectic and down-to-the-wire role, was '*how the gentlemen liked to take their tea.*' It was a task that women, no matter how senior or well-respected, were still expected to undertake. Only a short time into her job, Olive fell pregnant. Unmarried and committed to her career, she travelled to Essex for an abortion. Abortion was still illegal, and the procedure was almost fatal; she recovered in a nursing home in Manchester.

'But mother, I hate the wireless.'

It was a relief to Olive when, in 1937, she was promoted to the role of assistant producer away from *Children's Hour*. In her new job, Olive produced social documentaries revolving around the lives and labours of people in the north. She had worked on projects like this before: one of her first assignments at the BBC had been interviewing miners from County Durham. Her task was to hold up a large cardboard sign reading: 'No bloody or bugger', to remind the men not to swear in their interviews. This proved almost impossible, and they quickly gave up, battling to have the swearing kept in.

These were the people that Olive knew it was important to speak to in order to record and capture their stories. As she said: *'I wanted to have what I called "real people."'* Perhaps this came from her early political leanings, or perhaps just a simple, genuine interest in lives beyond those of the middle class. But her documentaries cut through a simple truth - that much of radio was staged, a drama, a warm picture of British life. It's understandable why the production teams in the north, and other regions, saw a chance to challenge this concept.

It was through making these documentaries that Olive's long love-affair with Manchester and the north began. Olive revolutionised interview techniques by taking recording equipment out to towns and cities in a twenty-mile-an-hour recording van, that was twenty-seven feet in length and weighed seven tonnes. This equipment gave Olive the freedom to create intimate and personal documentaries, taking listeners into the heart of miners' sitting rooms or busy, market town streets. Olive made documentaries on miners' wives, homelessness, long-distance truck drivers and canal journeying. Her voice, as noted in the leaked announcement, was known to millions. On her engagement to John Salt, the north regional programme director, Olive had to resign from her position at the BBC, but she could remain in a contracted position.

On the outbreak of the Second World War, Olive continued to make documentaries for the BBC, before moving with John to America, where he had been offered the job of deputy North American director. They left in 1941 and set up home in New York, staying in the home of British journalist Alistair Cooke. Olive sent newsletters back to *Children's Hour* about life in America and produced a series about 'real people' in the city. The first of these was composed of interviews with her black maid, Mabel Dobson, who advocated for the contributions made by BME communities to the war effort. Olive carried on making programmes whilst going through therapy for what we would today class as depression and anxiety, immediately after the birth of her first child. The family moved back to Manchester in 1945, resuming their work with the north region, but tragedy struck; after three children together and the makings of an incredibly happy and supportive home, John died of stomach cancer. It took Olive a long time to recover from this, but eventually she returned to broadcasting and the world she loved.

Juggling her burgeoning career, motherhood, and the grief of her loss, Olive became the presenter of *Woman's Hour* in 1949 and was one of the first presenters to tackle subjects such as the menopause and sexually transmitted diseases. Olive remained on *Woman's Hour* for over twenty years, identifying and interviewing some of the most forward-thinking and impressive women in the country.

Even after she had remarried, Olive's life never seemed to slow down. The family moved to Rose Hill, a large Victorian house in Didsbury. Olive suffered a severe nervous breakdown after the death of her second husband and recovered in Cheadle Royal Hospital. It was here when approaching retirement, that she decided to use the large house for good and subsequently turned the house into a refuge for unmarried mothers. Olive attributed the inspiration for this to her Aunt Alice:

'She was matron of a home for unmarried mothers…at the time, associating with married mothers must have been akin to Christ's associating with the lepers. Several decades later, I myself was to provide shelter at my house…for women in a similar position. Perhaps Aunt Alice's ghost was watching over me even then. But also, unconventional as I was, I just felt this was the right thing to do.'

Unconventional, yes – Olive Shapley's life was full of bold moves, determined career steps and courage in the face of tragedy and in short, the makings of a thoroughly modern woman. Olive's visionary broadcasting talents led to the voices of normal people making their way onto the radio and she single-handedly opened the eyes and ears of the nation to different ways of living, from the poor to the unusual. Olive may not have been from Manchester, but it was undoubtedly her home and she bore all the trademarks of a radical and inspiring Mancunian woman.

'If civilisation is to advance at all in the future, it must be through the help of women, women freed of their political shackles.'

As the statue of Emmeline Pankhurst perhaps demonstrates, the fight for votes for women has remained at the heart of public memory and at the mention of radical or campaigning women, the fight for women's suffrage is often brought to the forefront of the conversation. The white, green and purple of the centenary celebrations in 2018 also demonstrate the prominence of militant suffrage in campaigning memory. And yet, women's enfranchisement was just one small part of the radical efforts women made to free themselves of certain social restrictions. Women were barely able to own property, banned from graduating from university and from an early age at school, domestic disciplines were prioritised over academic ones. From this young age, they were primed to be wives and mothers, not active or engaged citizens.

As a registrar in the city, Emmeline Pankhurst was repeatedly reminded of the bonds placed on women, especially working-class women, to prevent them from advancing in society. In 1900, when she took a place on the Board of Education she wrote:

'I needed only one more experience…
to convince me that if civilisation is to advance at all in the future, it must be through the help of women, women freed of their political shackles, women to work their will in society.'

Through the long-list so far, we have explored the lives of suffragists and suffragettes, of artists and cultural pioneers, and of women who fought for the rights of the working-class woman. Here, we examine the lives of women who, despite being tied (as Emmeline Pankhurst described it) by political shackles and social restrictions, fought tirelessly to educate the nation on the social freedoms that not only women, but all of society deserved. From modern housing, proper education, to the long and painful fight against racism, the women in this section carried on the fight for social justice and equality once the vote had already been won.

Marie Stopes, Shena Simon, Kathleen Ollerenshaw and Louise Da-Cocodia all prove what happened when women were able to 'work their will' in society and subsequently the work of these four women spread further than their original roots in Manchester. This city is perhaps one of the few commonalities between these four women, as they carried out their work using different methods. At the heart of it all, however, was education and learning. Each of these women, in their own way, sought to shape the learning devices and teaching approaches of the nation.

For **Marie Stopes**, the first woman to be appointed a lecturer of sciences at the University of Manchester, educating the nation on sex and proper birth control was her life-long crusade. She believed that relief from constant pregnancies and a proper understanding of the mystery of sex would liberate women to fulfil their further potentials. Marie was, and remains, a controversial and difficult character within Manchester's canon of radical women, which is explored in more depth later. Marie would never have had the platform she did without her early access to higher education.

For many young women, this was not only a place for further learning and a new route to securing a career, but a place to become socially and politically liberated. Looking through the long-list, many of the women here benefited from a higher education. Esther Roper was one of the first women to attend Owen's College in Manchester, whilst Ellen Wilkinson, whose time at the University of Manchester gave her access to socialist and left-leaning societies and clubs, became the first female Minister of Education in 1941.

Equally, **Shena Simon** and **Kathleen Ollerenshaw** both attended women-only colleges at Cambridge and Oxford respectively and both ended up sitting on the Education Committee as city councillors, determined to improve access to education and education for girls in the city. Before them, Margaret Ashton had sat on the Education Committee until she had been removed due to her anti-war sentiment in 1917.

Louise Da-Cocodia did not have the same access to higher education, and her social activism sits beyond the parameters of education, yet despite this, the Louise Da-Cocodia Education Trust was launched on 2008. As a legacy of the work she carried out improving race relations in the city and supporting young black communities, the Education Trust provides a supplementary school for BME students and financial support for BME higher education students studying business, sciences, technology and engineering. It now encompasses a wide-range of projects, including summer schools and programmes for students at risk of exclusion.

Louise had a long and illustrious career, becoming the first black senior nursing officer in Greater Manchester and a prolific campaigner against racism and bigotry. From her own experiences as a young woman during her nurses training, Louise recognised the support needed for young people to grow and achieve, as she said:

'Young Black people need role models around, not necessarily high-profile ones… You can get what you want through hard work and determination, even with the prejudice that they will face from time to time. This is my honest belief.'

These four women were able to bring about social change through education – and in Louise's case, were able to create opportunities for education through social enterprise. They challenge the perception of 'first in the fight' – indeed, they highlight just how many more 'fights' are left to be won. Louise's fight in particular, is still far from being over. However, as long as there are people like Louise, like Kathleen, like Shena, who will advocate for better education and promote a tolerant, equal and liberated society, the fight may be won sooner, rather than later.

"Every heart desires a mate."

Marie Charlotte Carmichael Stopes • 1880 – 1958

MARIE STOPES

The radical and revolutionary women of Manchester are not always native to the city. Some, like Marie Stopes, found their cause and calling in the city, leading them to create moments of radical and powerful social change. For Marie Stopes, Manchester was the place where she would fight to teach women about contraception and have a better understanding of sex. Her book, Married Love, caused both sensation and outcry when it was released in 1918.

It was based, in large, on her own experiences in her first marriage and the sexual frustrations she held. As she wrote in the preface:

'In my own marriage I paid such a terrible price for sex-ignorance that I feel that knowledge gained at such a cost should be placed at the service of humanity.'

Marie Stopes' story often highlights the problematic narratives that surround some people in history, and indeed, the problem with making somebody into a statue. We often celebrate a singular moment or action in somebody's long life, sometimes leading us to forget, or ignore, the other aspects of their story; Marie's life story highlights the consequences of this. Marie Stopes fought for birth control, confronted the social restrictions of sex and opened the country's eyes to understanding sex and contraception from the point of view of a woman. However, she also held some opinions about eugenics and race that both today, and in the early 20th century, were considered controversial.

Marie Stopes was born on 15th October 1880, in Edinburgh. Her father came from a wealthy brewing family, but held a passion for archaeology and palaeontology that his daughter would inherit. Whilst Marie's childhood was stereotypical for a family of her class, a world away from the radical drawing rooms that fellow future revolutionary women were exposed to, she did have some early radical influences. Marie's mother, Charlotte, was a prominent campaigner for women's education, a renowned Shakespeare scholar and had been an early campaigner against corsets. If she had, like her daughter, ended up with a close connection to Manchester, she herself may have been considered as the subject for the statue. Unsurprisingly, Charlotte was also a member of the National Union of Women's Suffrage Societies (NUWSS). It's probable Marie learnt early on that social obligations and norms for women could be flexed and fought against, from the campaigning that Charlotte carried out under their roof.

Marie was an intelligent child who never faced the struggle for education many other young, poorer women faced. Alongside her sister, Winnie, Marie was educated at first in Edinburgh and later in London, when the family moved. Considering her father's scientific background and her mother's championing of female education, it seemed unimaginable that Marie would not pursue higher education. She enrolled at University College London in 1900, where she excelled, taking a degree in biology and geology and graduating with a first-class honours degree two years later. This itself was an extraordinary feat and she wrote to her family of the failure of her fellow male students to achieve anything close to what she had done. She undertook her PhD in Munich, becoming the first woman to achieve a PhD in Botany at the university there. Marie was undoubtedly a driven intellectual, widely renowned for her academic achievements. Upon her qualification and return home, Dr Marie Stopes made a name for herself as the youngest Doctor of Science in Britain.

At this stage, Marie did not begin to turn her entire life to sexual revolution, as she soon would do. Instead she focused on academia, becoming the first female lecturer in the sciences at the University of Manchester, specialising in paleo-botany, a study of extinct plant life. Although the university panicked and tried to redact the appointment upon realising that Dr Stopes was a woman, they were unsuccessful. Marie's career flourished and she travelled across the world on expeditions to Japan and Canada, balancing her teaching with her travels. Romance blossomed in Tokyo when Marie was reconciled with an acquaintance from Munich, Dr Kenjiro Fujii. Fujii was married and the relationship fell apart; a scorned Marie returned home. These early adventures of Marie's are telling of her character and her later activism; she truly broke the mould of what a young woman should do, think and say.

Marie first married in 1911, to fellow scientist Reginald Gates, whom she had met whilst working in Canada. The marriage was troubled, marred by Reginald's resentment of Marie's career and his jealousy of her close relationship with their lodger. The marriage remained unconsummated and was annulled on those grounds in 1916. She remarried businessman, Humphrey Roe in 1918. Humphrey was an early supporter of the birth control movement and provided the capital needed for Marie's first book to be published. Marie gave birth to their son, Harry Stopes-Roe, in 1924. She adored her only child and aimed to protect him at all costs – though it would cause the end of their relationship further down the line.

In the same year that she gave birth, Marie published her book, *Married Love*. The book was a roaring success, despite struggling to find a publishing house to publish it and sold out within weeks. From kitchen maids to mistresses of the household, women everywhere secretly devoured the tome, finally relishing in a book that understood their sexuality and sexual needs. Marie drew on experiences from her first marriage and what she had been able to teach herself from her books – specifically the lack of attention given to female desire and stimulation. As she wrote:

'Consequently woman's side of the sexual life has found little or no expression. Woman has been content to mold herself to the shape desired by man wherever possible, and she has stifled her natural feelings and her own deep thoughts as they welled up.'

Married Love aimed to take away the stigmas and the shame surrounding women's sexuality, writing:

'The idea that woman is lowered or "soiled" by sexual intercourse is still deeply rooted in some strata of our society.'

Historically, a sexually active woman – especially an openly sexually active woman – was considered unclean and acting outside of the social norms. Marie used *Married Love* to challenge this, blaming the double standards for the problems many young couples suffered when they consummated their marriage.

Married Love made Marie Stopes a household name and gained her some sizable enemies, who claimed her work was pornographic and morally wrong. One church critic accused her of: 'deliberate cultivation of sexual union as an end unto itself…', and of celebrating the pleasures of sex, rather than the moral ideals of sex, which was to merely reproduce.

This didn't stop her from continuing her career and advocacy. As she argued for sexual liberation and understanding, she moved onto advocating for birth control and contraceptives. At the time, this was incredibly dangerous; early advocates for birth control had been arrested and tried for obscene libel. But Marie continued to write, including a pamphlet published in 1919 for working-class women, called *A Letter to Working Mothers*. Inklings of Marie's controversial opinions on eugenics and sterilisation appear in this pamphlet, but overall, the message was clear – unwanted pregnancies were dangerous for women. Marie identified the lack of sex education as the cause of these unwanted pregnancies, arguing the more children in the family, the weaker, hungrier and sicker these children would be. She pushed for the use of contraceptives such as pessaries and condoms, and on 17th March 1921, opened the first Birth Control Clinic in Holloway. The clinic was supported by the Society for Constructive Birth Control that Marie had founded earlier that year. At these clinics, women had access to contraceptives and advice on the most effective methods of birth control. Stopes did not support all forms of contraception and did not agree with abortion, preferring to champion other devices (some of her own design) that would prevent this final, illegal and dangerous procedure.

As Marie's infamy grew and her work became internationally renowned, so did her controversies. She was known to be difficult to work with, and was described by many, including her son, as an egomaniac, believing she was the key to solving problems such as poverty and inequality across the world.

Despite being a prolific author, playwright and scientist, Marie's radicalism became a source of controversy. She expressed opinions that both then and now are considered contentious. Marie had been a member of the Eugenics Society since 1912 and became a fierce advocate of it, arguing that it would help to prevent a surplus of children being born into poverty. However, eugenics even then held negative connotations and links to racial cleansing. Eventually, these differing beliefs created enough tension within the Society for Constructive Birth Control that Marie split from the organisation. It was a disturbing belief; she wrote in a later article: 'We must breed for quality, not for quantity…' Marie would later disinherit her only son for marrying a woman who needed to wear glasses, believing it to be a genetic defect.

Despite this, Marie's name still lends itself to birth control and sexual health clinics around the world. Marie Stopes International is an organisation that now provides free contraception and safe abortions to women all around the world, continuing at least a part of Marie's interesting and unique legacy.

Marie was a fierce feminist, although her troubling beliefs have made her a difficult heroine for our times. She supported women's suffrage, advocated for equal pay in the workplace, as well as better education for women. Without Marie's support of better birth control, sexual liberation for women and education on the biology and emotions of sex, the birth control movement would never have advanced at the speed that it did - for that, we must thank her. Although many of her ideas were extreme and incredibly ill-judged, she truly believed that everything she did, she did for the well-being of women.

SHENA SIMON

Although the textile industry that fueled Manchester's prosperity was predominantly made up of female workers, the home was undeniably the domain of the woman. For both working women and housewives, the responsibility of looking after the house, cleaning, cooking and often managing the finances was left to them. Women who worked had to manage their housework around their long, working hours. It is no wonder that, in the 20th century, social and private housing went through rigorous changes to improve and implement modern commodities that would make the work around the house easier. In Manchester, one of the solutions to clear slums and provide better social housing lay in Wythenshawe, a place which some councillors and social reformers had identified as the perfect location for a green suburbia for the working classes. The building scheme would provide:

'…for every woman a clean, well-planned home, which will be her palace – so well and wisely planned that her labour will be lightened and her strength and intelligence reserved for wider interests.'

What those broader interests were could be summarised by all the things that Shena Simon championed - active citizenship for women and better education. Indeed the driving force behind the Wythenshawe Scheme were Shena Dorothy Simon and her husband Ernest (the latter being the MP for Withington). Both were prolific liberals and progressives in the city, who had long been concerned by the living conditions of the working class. Shena's name is not always remembered in Manchester. She ran parallel, perhaps, to Ellen Wilkinson in her political leanings and her commitment to better education for women. However, she did not have the same firebrand identity that Ellen had cultivated and had always led a life of relative privilege. However, Shena was an important political figure in Manchester, and in a world where some women were finally able to vote, carried on the fight for social equality for women.

Of course, Shena was in a position to be able to do this without restraint. She was born Dorothy Shena Potter into an affluent household in Surrey on 21st October 1883. Her father was a shipowner and her brothers all worked for his company whilst Shena, as she was known, and her sisters were given a traditional education expected of middle-class women. Shena, however, must have shown some educational prowess, as she went up to Newnham College, Cambridge to study economics, before attending London School of Ecomonics to continue her studies to postgraduate level.

Her interest in liberal politics was deepened during this period and she joined the National Union for Women Workers, alongside her political idol, Margaret MacDonald. Margaret was the wife of eventual Labour leader and the first Labour Prime Minister Ramsay MacDonald, and was, in her own right, a powerful and prominent social campaigner. Shena would have learnt a great deal from Margaret and the other women in the union, but it was not in London where she would continue her political journey, but in Manchester, the home of radical reform.

Shena may never have visited Manchester if it had not been for a weekend visit to her friend from university, Eva Hubback, who had recently moved following her marriage to a lecturer at the University of Manchester. Eva was a friend of the Simon family – a progressive, industrialist family from Didsbury, and she had a suspicion that Shena would be more than a match for Ernest, their socialist son, who had recently taken over the family business. Ernest later described meeting Shena as a: '…purely mental attraction.' Both had found the person who understood their politics and their outlook on the world, and they were instantly attracted to each other. In November 1912, Ernest and Shena were married; they honeymooned in Italy and returned to make a home in Manchester. The Simons socialised with a liberal group of friends, including the Scott family (C.P Scott was the editor of Manchester Guardian) and lecturers from the University of Manchester.

It didn't take long for Shena to throw herself into the political realm that her husband also occupied. Ernest was a councillor on Manchester City Council and sat on several committees across the city. In the years following their marriage, Shena balanced her political career with the birth of her three children, supported by a household of domestic servants and support. Her perpetual domestic bliss was blighted with tragedy in 1929 when her daughter, only twelve years old, died of cancer.

Shena had always supported women's suffrage and had been a supporter of the WSPU, having been a fan of Emmeline Pankhurst. Her parents had disapproved of the radical actions of the WSPU, and she had to come to a compromise, writing:

'I made a bargain with them that if they let me to speak and walk in processions etc, I would not do anything actively militant.'

Shena's absence from the 1911 census when she was living in London, suggests she was amongst those suffrage campaigners who boycotted the census, as they believed those who didn't count politically should not be counted socially. Despite supporting the WSPU, she continued to campaign. During the troubled and distressing times of the First World War, she founded the Manchester and Salford Women's Citizen Association. (WCA). Militant activity had accelerated before war had broken out and women were taking an active place in the workforce as men went off to fight. The WCA offered a place for women (who were still unable to vote) to understand and learn how they could be active citizens, outside of fighting for the vote. The association encouraged women to use their voice in debates around child welfare, pensions, housing and health. It was a broader feminist movement that sustained throughout the war and joined with its fellow franchises to form the National Women's Citizen Association in 1917.

Shena's predominant interest was in education, and after the war this was where she turned her attention. Ernest had become the youngest Lord Mayor of Manchester in 1921. Shena used the position of Lady Mayoress to her advantage, visiting many schools to inspect and examine the conditions of education. She notably refused to attend a function at St Mary's Hospital for Women because no women actually sat on the board, nor were there any female staff members.

In 1924, Shena took her political action further when she, like her husband years before, was elected to Manchester City Council and in 1932 became part of the Education Committee. She fought against cuts to education, for the abolition of school fees, for comprehensive schools and successfully campaigned for married women to remain in their posts as teachers. She strongly believed that education should be for all and not be divided by class or gender. Even after she was voted off the council by the Conservative Party, she remained as a co-opted member and did her best to prevent any cuts, or anything that would end the work she had started in her time there.

Alongside the work she carried out for improving education, she was invested in improving housing conditions across the city, as her work in Wythenshawe demonstrates. The houses on the new estate had running water, baths and gardens, and were designed so that women's domestic duties would be much easier (despite the longer trips to the shops).

Shena and Ernest bought Wythenshawe Hall and Park from the Tatton family in 1926 as the new estate was being developed. They gifted it back to the city, stating it must:

'…be kept forever as an open space for the people of Manchester.'

Ernest was knighted in 1932, making Shena Lady Simon of Wythenshawe. Still, Shena continued to advocate for educational change and in the following years, set up both the Association for Education in Citizenship and the Council for Educational Advance. She supported the 1944 Education Act, which, amongst other things, raised the school leaving age and reformed secondary education. Shena's influence was visible in the sector until her retirement.

Like many of the other women on this list, Shena had the financial freedom to dedicate her time to activism and change. Unlike her fellow educationalist, Ellen Wilkinson (who would become the first female Minister of Education in 1945), Shena never experienced a working-class upbringing and couldn't necessarily empathise with the women who she supported with such vigour. Still, her work helped to change the social landscape of the city in the inter-war period and left a long-standing legacy of tenacity and the belief that improving housing, education, and social benefits would lead to a brighter future. Shena passed away on 17th July 1972. Her commitment to education was memorialised in the Shena Simon campus at the Manchester College.

KATHLEEN OLLERENSHAW

Remembered as one of the greatest mathematicians in the country, Kathleen's own education steered her towards an incredible career at a time when the role of the woman was still firmly placed in the household. A native Mancunian, Kathleen remained in the city for most of her life and balanced her academic career with her a long-standing role on the City Council and her family life. After a childhood illness Kathleen was almost fully deaf from a young age and despite facing prejudice and lack of provision for this, she was determined this would never stand in her way and ended her career in 10 Downing Street, advising Britain's first female Prime Minister.

Kathleen was born in Withington at 1 Parkgate Avenue, on 1st October 1912. Her father, Charles Timpson, was the son of Timpsons founder William Timpson, a boot repairer and manufacturer. She lived with her father, her mother Mary and her sister Betty, as well as Laura, their servant. Kathleen noted in her autobiography how much she adored this house and her pleasant, happy upbringing. Her father was the president of the Local Liberal Association and was, and interested in and on the periphery of, local politics.

Kathleen never knew where her love of numbers came from, but she reflected in her autobiography, *To Talk Of Many Things*, that it was visible early on; she describes reading her favourite childhood book, *Peter Rabbit*, and counting the brass buttons on his vest. Her family recognised her intellect and her skill with sums, but Kathleen noted that her mother never quite understood it, frequently making comments such as:

'Why are you doing those sums again, when you haven't shelled the peas?'

Mary had been the eldest daughter in a crowded Victorian family and was therefore denied an education so she could remain at home and care for her younger siblings. Although she felt uneasy at Kathleen's prowess, it didn't deter her from sending both Betty and Kathleen to the Montessori Ladybarn House School, encouraged by the fact that *Manchester Guardian* editor CP Scott sent his children there. She became close friends with a fellow student here, Robert Ollerenshaw, who lived half way between her house and the school. In To Talk Of Many Things, she reflects fondly on him becoming her childhood sweetheart:

'I have a snapshot taken…at his 7th birthday party. He has his arm around my shoulder as if I was the only girl in the world.'

Illustration by **Alex Francis**

111

Kathleen excelled at school and was encouraged particularly by her school mistress Miss Ratalick, who was, Kathleen recalled, gifted at mathematics beyond the usual arithmancy. As she was flourishing so much it must have been a blow when, aged eight, she caught a cold during a summer holiday in Anglesey. This rendered her part deaf and a family genetic condition, otosclerosis, worsened the situation meaning she was almost fully deaf by the age of twelve. Professor Alexander Ewing at the University of Manchester specialised in lip-reading and believed that sign-language was redundant, with lip-reading being a more universally effective way of communication. And so, Kathleen was instructed on lip-reading, becoming Ewing's 'star pupil'; indeed, Kathleen could lip-read so effectively barely any of her peers knew of her disability. Kathleen attributes her passion for mathematics to her deafness; as she wrote in her autobiography:

'Nearly all mathematic equations and diagrams are found in books or are shown on a blackboard as the teacher speaks. Answers are written down. Learning mathematics is rarely as dependent on the spoken word…'

Kathleen was then sent to the prestigious boarding school, St Leonards in St Andrews. Although she enjoyed the school and shone at sport, she was restricted when it came to taking her School Certificate and did not take physics or chemistry to further study. Her science teacher was so cruel about her deafness, refusing to repeat missed statements or give her any allowance in class – Kathleen, terrified, regretted dropping the subjects for the rest of her life. Throughout, mathematics was a constant and she was encouraged by Robert, who sent her his side-ruler as he believed she would go further into mathematics than he would. He was right.

Kathleen spent a year being tutored by Professor Child at the University of Manchester, before taking the Oxford and Cambridge entrance exams. She struggled with the Cambridge interview and, on sharing that she was deaf with the interviewers, felt this had disadvantaged her. She didn't reveal her deafness in her Oxford interview. Although she was offered places at both (Cambridge, she wrote in her autobiography, seemed to offer it with a degree of reluctance), she decided to study at Oxford. Kathleen took a place at Somerville College in 1930. Robert was there studying physiology and in her first term the two became engaged. There was no mathematics tutor at the college, so she had to go to a tutor at Balliol for her studies.

Kathleen was a keen sportsperson and spent much of her time as an undergraduate occupying herself with sporting or social events, becoming hockey captain and attending dances across the university. She left with a first-class degree (although she was still unable to graduate) and began work at the Shirley Institute, a cotton research centre in Manchester, where she applied her skills in statistics. Her work included the study of water-proofing kits for the military. She was granted a permanent position at the institute, but left after the birth of her son.

After her marriage to Robert in 1939, before he was called up to fight in the Second World War, Kathleen gave up her job to run the house; although she moved back to her parents' home during the war, as she could not hear the air raid sirens. Kathleen still remained dedicated to her mathematical work, committing her study to critical lattice and returned to Oxford in 1943. She completed her PhD back at Somerville in 1945, publishing more than five papers in three years. Whilst raising her two children, Charles and Florence and with her husband fighting overseas, she continued employment as a part-time lecturer at the University of Manchester.

Kathleen was one of the first people in the country to receive a hearing aid, which, despite being horribly uncomfortable, she described as: *'one of the greatest blessings I could imagine was granted to me.'* For the first time in many years, she could hear almost perfectly.

Throughout her career, Kathleen published over thirty articles on critical lattices and her later interest, magic squares. In later life, Kathleen was one of the first people to solve the Rubik's Cube, working out an algorithm to solve it in only eighty moves. Her long-standing fascination with astronomy led to her becoming the vice-president of the Manchester Astronomical Society.

An observatory at the University of Lancaster is named after her, after she donated one of her telescopes.

Her passion for learning and her commitment to teaching was lauded nationally and Kathleen travelled the country giving lectures on mathematics. Her interest in politics arose from an interest in education, particularly for girls, and the conditions of schools across Greater Manchester. Elected as a Conservative councillor in 1956, Kathleen joined the Manchester Education Committee and became chairperson of the Association of Governing Bodies of Girls' Public Schools. She published *Education for Girls* in 1961 and continued to advocate for better schooling for girls and access to an education beyond domestic subjects. She was almost voted from the committee by the Labour Party in 1966, but fought to keep her place, with the support of the many academic institutions she supported. Kathleen remained a councillor for twenty-six years and whilst her voice was heard and respected both nationally and internationally, she remained dedicated to the welfare of Manchester and never left the city.

Kathleen's services to education were recognised in 1970 when she was awarded an MBE and Manchester followed suit when she was made Lord Mayor of Manchester in 1975. Forever committed to the city, it was through Kathleen's efforts that the Royal Northern College of Music was created through the merging of two music schools. As well as a wealth of honorary degrees, Kathleen sat on the governing board of five universities throughout her career and later advised on educational matters to the cabinet of the first female Prime Minister, Margaret Thatcher.

Her extensive catalogue of honours and achievements are almost too long to list, but they were all earned through tireless work and effort, despite personal tragedies and the struggle with her hearing. She achieved the highest honour of the city in 1984, when she was awarded the Freedom of the City. Everything she did throughout her long and celebrated life aimed to help others. In her own words:

'It is not surprising that, when aged forty I first had hearing aids and a little later found myself in public life, everything gradually became centred on the endeavour to help others as far as possible, to let them have the same opportunities as myself.'

Kathleen passed away on 10th August 2014 at her home in Didsbury. One of her final roles in the city had been as a patron for the Museum of Science and Industry, as it was known when it opened in 2003. It seems fitting that a place designed to bring knowledge, interest and joy to young people across Greater Manchester was one of her final contributions to the city that she gave so much to.

LOUISE DA-COCODIA

'I am because we are' is an old African proverb, that, after travelling across seas and countries, fits easily into the culture of Manchester. It is the concept of a bond that ties humanity together, allowing us to flourish as one. Manchester, a city based on togetherness and prosperity in the unity of a worker bees' hive embodies this proverb. It is no wonder that Louise Da Cocodia, a prominent activist, nurse and anti-racism campaigner, adopted the proverb as her own personal saying and she dedicated her life to community action and representing young black people across the city. Her eminent career with the National Health Service (NHS) came at a time when prejudices within the NHS were deep-rooted against people of colour.

Louise's story is as rousing and inspiring as the other nineteen women; however, her place on this list holds another importance. Louise was the only woman of colour long-listed for the statue, which seems somewhat strange for such a diverse, multi-cultural city. In some ways, Louise represents those stories missing from the list and the women who are not included. It isn't a role she should have to undertake. It feels almost fitting, if not a little ironic, that the Louise Da-Cocodia Education Trust runs a heritage project named Women of the Soil, celebrating black women across Manchester.

Louise was born on 9th November 1934, as Louse Wright in the St Catherine's Parish of Jamaica, thirty miles outside of Kingston. Her father was a railway foreman and their household was run in adherence to strict religious morals. She attended an equally disciplined school in Kingston and achieved her School Certificate there. We don't know when Louise decided she would become a nurse, but it was an extremely over-subscribed profession in Jamaica, with a long waiting list. Like many other young women, Louise decided to move to England to complete her training as a nurse. This was not unusual; women from the Caribbean colonies had served as nurses during World War Two and with the birth of the National Health Service (NHS) in 1948, more nurses were needed to fill hospitals across the country.

Louise was part of the Windrush generation, referring to a mass migration of people from the Caribbean to the UK during the 1940s and 1950s. The name derived from the Empire Windrush, a ship that brought over hundreds of people in 1948 – the first of many. The 1948 British Nationality Act granted citizenship to anybody arriving from the Empire. People across the Empire had contributed to the war effort in World War Two and over one hundred thousand men from the Caribbean were signed up to fight for the Allied Forces. Women joined the Auxiliary Territorial Services and the Auxiliary Air Force. These servicemen and servicewomen often received racial abuse from their peers and from members of the public; some men were even rejected from the army because of the colour of their skin.

Illustration by **Ellie Thomas**

Whilst young women were encouraged by the British government to make the journey overseas, they had to fund their own places, despite the government creating several schemes to assist with the cost of travel. Adapting to life in the UK was a huge upheaval for many. The government released pamphlets to try and assist with this change, with advice on dressing for the climate and what accommodation to look for, but these were little comfort. Like many of the women, Louise may have assumed she would return to her home after completing her training, but, like her fellow nurses, remained and made a life for herself in the UK. In 1951, she arrived to train in St Olaves Hospital, London. Here, Louise trained as a State Registered Nurse, a qualification that she was fortunate to receive, as many other Caribbean women who came to qualify were trained to become State Enrolled Nurses, which was a lower qualification.

The NHS depended on nurses like Louise, but later in life she recalled the treatment she received from her colleagues and patients. Black and Irish nurses were given the menial jobs; during Louise's training, she remembered being giving the job of 'sluicing', which she described as washing the waste of incontinent patients. Irish and black nurses were made to do this and then wash the dirty sheets in a freezing cold washroom, but complaining was futile – nobody would admit to the racial prejudices that were prevalent throughout the NHS. Patients, too, were often averse to having a black nurse. Louise recalled times when she was bathing patients who would tell her: '... keep your dirty hands off me!' Louise pointed out the irony in this, giving that she was cleaning the patients because they themselves were unclean. Other nurses reported that they would have faeces thrown at them by patients. Even doctors were reported to bypass more qualified nurses and speak directly to white nurses.

In 1963, Louise qualified as a nurse and subsequently carried out midwifery and health visitor training. She was the only black student midwife on her course but did not allow any of the prejudices she continued to receive to deter her. Midwifery and the care of women both pre- and post-natal was a skilled role that had to be carried out with care and precision and one in which Louise would come across women from all walks of life. She met her husband, Ted, whilst he was studying Law in Manchester and they were married in 1964. Two years later, Louise became the assistant superintendent of District Nurses in Manchester, running a large team of health visitors and nurses. Even in this senior position, Louise was faced with discrimination and she recounted overhearing one of her nurses mutter: '*These black so-and-so's, coming over and telling us all what to do*', under her breath as she walked away from her.

Facing these racial slurs and bigotry on a daily basis no doubt encouraged Louise's involvement in tackling racism. The Race Relations Act was passed in 1965, banning discrimination on '*the grounds of colour, race, or ethnic or national origins*'. Following this, the 1968 Race Relations Act made discrimination in employment, housing and advertising illegal also. Race Relations boards were set up at a national level but were rarely utilised and racism and bigotry still prevailed in society. Alongside working full-time in her senior nursing role and raising her children, Louise became a member of the regional Race Relations Board and the West Indian Organisation Co-ordinating Committee (WIOCC). The WIOCC was founded by Eloise and Nana Edwards in 1964 and brought together several organisations in the city to provide community support and advice for West Indian communities in the city, particularly for young people. All who remember Louise speak of her warm, humorous and kind personality, the beating heart of the community. This, as Brian Robson described, was one of her greatest strengths; combining '*...the formal with the informal, the community with the committee.*' It is no surprise, then, that Louise was invited to sit on several community boards and committees across the city, all with an aim to improve race relations and advocate for BME communities.

As she said herself, these actions were driven by the unjust and unfair treatment of black people, despite the Race Relations act. As she said:

'Deep in my mind is my commitment to bridge the gap which has led to the blacks being treated as inferior.'

In 1981, racial tensions mounted in Manchester and resulted in the Moss Side Riots. Beset with unemployment, the young black community in Moss Side were often subjected to 'stop and search' tactics by the police. The inquiry into the riots were deemed biased as they placed the blame solely on young black men, ignoring reports from witnesses contradicting this. The Moss Side Defence Committee was formed to support the young people who had been arrested during the riots, but they boycotted the inquiry. Louise, having driven injured parties from the riots to hospital, had been invited to sit on the inquiry panel. She believed her role on the inquiry board would be a positive influence and help steer the board away from racial bias or prejudice – to do this, she had to resign from the Defence Committee. The events of 1981 demonstrated how much Manchester, famed for its progression and radicalism, still had problems with racism and still needed to change.

Louise retired from nursing in 1989 as a senior nursing officer. It had been a long and impressive career, during which she had been the first senior black nurse in the city and had advocated for equal treatment of BME nurses in the profession, even publishing a paper on the subject in 1984. Once retired, she dedicated her time wholly to her community work in Manchester. Louise had long been a part of the Walton Housing Association, which offered housing care and advice, educational and childcare support and courses and activities for the West Indian community. In the aftermath of the Moss Side riots,

Louise recognised the importance for more housing support and formed the Arawak Housing Association, which offered specialist support for older generations and communities. Aside from housing advice, they worked to combat loneliness in the community, to tackle financial worries and support with health advice. At the helm of it all was Louise, who acted as the first chair. Known affectionately as Mrs D, she remained a well-known and respected figure in the Moss Side community, where she worked tirelessly to break down social barriers not only for the young, but the elderly too. Alongside becoming a Justice of the Peace, she became the chair of the Moss Side and Hulme Women's Action Forum and formed Cariocca Enterprises. This was another of her social initiatives, giving business support and advice to young people starting their own businesses and start-ups.

Louise's services to the BME communities and her commitment to improving race relations across Manchester were recognised first with the Manchester Race Award, an honorary degree from the University of Manchester, and, in 2005, an MBE for her community work. She became a deputy lord lieutenant for Greater Manchester in 1999. Louise passed away on 13th March 2008, but her legacy lives on. The Cariocca Education Trust, a strand of Cariocca Enterprises, was renamed the Louise Da-Cocodia Education Trust. Their mission statement sums up Louise's entire life's work: *'To provide relevant and accessible education, employment and enterprise services, in particular to people of African and Caribbean heritage, so they can fulfil their potential and achieve their aspirations.'*

Louise was an incredible force within the community and with her positive, determined attitude, did a remarkable amount for race relations in Manchester. She stands shoulder to shoulder with many other anti-racism campaigners who, from WIOCC founder Eloise Edwards to anti-gun campaigner Erinma Bell, have fought to make Manchester a tolerant, kind, and equal city.

'Don't say "I can't, for "I can't" never did anything. Say, at least, "I will try"– that works wonders. But oh, say "I will DO" – that works miracles.'

The final three women on the long-list come from three entirely different backgrounds and eras. One, an age when women's suffrage may have been privately whispered but never publicly asked for; the other, at a time when the country was caught in the throes of the fight for enfranchisement, and the third, after all women had been franchised under the Representation of the People (equal franchise) Act. Despite the continuous changes in social and political circumstance for women, there were still limitations and prejudices in place that women had to face. The idea that women couldn't do anything as well as men (or, indeed, at all), was a social acceptance that women were constantly having to face and overcome. The three women on this list all faced this bias and acted against it to absolute success, overcoming doubt and failure along the way. From demonstrating women's effectiveness within the charitable and scientific realm, to excelling at sporting achievements that, at one time, would have seemed impossible, these three women showed a tenacity comparable to Emmeline Pankhurst and her militant suffragettes. An article published in Votes for Women, the newspaper ran by Emmeline and Fredrick Pethwick-Lawrence in July 1913, published almost two hundred years after Elizabeth Raffald's book was published, two years after the birth of Sunny Lowry, and over twenty years after Emily Williamson founded the RSPB, seems to sum up their behaviour perfectly:

'Don't say "I can't, for "I can't" never did anything. Say, at least, "I will try" – that works wonders. But oh, say "I will DO" – that works miracles.'

Undoubtedly, these three women were women who said I will do. For some it was easier than others. 18th century cook, entrepreneur and author **Elizabeth Raffald** and Royal Society for the Protection of Birds (RSPB) founder **Emily Williamson** both succeeded by acting within the realms that women were able to take up space in: the domestic sphere and the world of charity and fundraising. Middle-class women were expected to play a part in these domains. Elizabeth, like her fellow authoress Elizabeth Gaskell, wrote books designed to capture the interests of women, but this should not take away from the sheer ingenuity and sharp thinking it must have taken to move from the role of housekeeper to entrepreneur. After publishing her nationally best-selling recipe book, Elizabeth built up an empire based on canny investments and insightful opportunities. Her sex did not prevent this, for her skills were deemed acceptable within the remit of what women were expected to do. There are no reports of her coming up against male adversity, although when the Raffalds opened their coffee house, it was John Raffald who was named the master, although it seems unlikely that John would be leading the enterprise due to his lack of business sense and his secondary role in the Raffald empire.

Emily Williamson refused to say *I can't*, and persevered when she refused to let pointless misogyny stop her from campaigning against the plumage trade. Emily, despite being a middle-class woman whose husband and father-in-law were already respected within the scientific world (one as an amateur, the other professionally), was herself barred from joining the British Ornithologists' Union (BOU) simply because she was a woman. This wasn't uncommon; despite women proving their intelligence in universities across the country, they were still deemed an anomaly of their sex, their learning often a distraction from their true purpose of raising a family and running a household. The idea that women could sustain intellectual debate and discussion was almost unfathomable; the idea that a woman would *want* to do this usurped societal ideas and was not to be encouraged. Women challenged this across the country and in 1896, Emily Williamson joined these women after being banned from the BOU. Her response of setting up her own society – which would become one of the biggest conservation charities

of the country – that refused men entry was perhaps the cutting wake-up call many needed to end the segregation of gender in intellectual organisations.

Even as society progressed, however, women still had to work twice as hard as men to be acknowledged, whilst facing more backlash for their accomplishments. Although in the sporting world women had been able to compete in different arenas for some time, there were still social restrictions for women. **Sunny Lowry's** experience is testament to this.

Sunny Lowry was not the first woman to swim the English channel and yet her achievement seems all the richer for the effort she put into it. Indeed, her story is the epitome of *I will do*. Sunny failed twice before she succeeded in swimming the channel. After crawling out of the sea victorious and flying the colours for hardy Manchester women, Sunny was still attacked for the choice of swimming costume that she wore – a two piece, instead of the accepted long swimsuit. Exposing her knees and her midriff seemed a small price to pay for what she achieved, yet the crowds on the beach where she had landed threatened to call the police, horrified at her indecency.

Doors did not begin to open simply because of changing times. They opened because of the women that said *I will do*; the women that hammered and shouted on the thresholds, demanding to be let in and the women who put a shoulder to the door frame, or a foot in the crack of a partially open door. Because of the women who ignored social convention and said *I will do*, businesses, organisations, law practices, sport and even educational facilities that had been previously shut off to them soon flourished because of the great minds and personalities now allowed to participate.

ELIZABETH RAFFALD

Before Mary Berry – indeed, even before Mrs Beeton - there was Elizabeth Raffald. In Exchange Square, a small plaque marks the site where Elizabeth, entrepreneur and developer, founded her first business. An often-hidden figure in Manchester, Elizabeth was not an advocate for women's suffrage, nor was she a player on the political stage. Instead, she transcended the ideals placed on women by demonstrating her mind for business and development. Elizabeth founded a business empire driven by her domestic skills and capitalised by her wily mind. From spotting good business opportunities to being incredibly canny at investing in new business, Elizabeth's name was once recognised across the nation as the authority on housekeeping and cooking.

Elizabeth was born Elizabeth Whittaker into an upper-working class family in Doncaster. Her father was a school teacher and whilst the education of young women was not considered useful for girls of her class, it is thanks to him that Elizabeth received a more robust education than most girls of her age, including learning how to speak French.

By the time she was fifteen, Elizabeth had entered into the life of domestic service. These roles, though often gruelling, exhausting, and lonely, were considered good and respectable working positions to have. Elizabeth stated she had served some of the 'great and worthy families' in the north and it was here that she recognised the skills needed – and the skills lacking – for many servants in the trade. The employment agency and her book would be borne from re-purposing and increasing the skills of servants and housekeepers alike.

It was at Arley Hall in Northwich, however, where Elizabeth's circumstances and fortunes would change. She was employed by Lady Elizabeth Warburton, the wife of the 4th Baronet. At the age of thirty, Elizabeth took on the prestigious and highly responsible role of housekeeper. Arley Hall was a quintessential stately home, with sprawling grounds, elegant gardens, a labyrinth of rooms and a family who required the highest quality and most dedicated service. Elizabeth, who had honed the fifteen years of experience she already had in the field, would have managed a vast number of female servants, including the house maids and the kitchen staff. Elizabeth's responsibilities at Arley Hall stretched to directing the table settings and decorations, as well as the show-stopping edible centrepieces, such as cakes and desserts.

At many houses, the housekeeping role was a post that would not have been given up lightly and many women would have kept the role until their retirement or marriage. Although thirty was a relatively late age to marry by the standards of the day, Elizabeth found romance at Arley Hall, and married the head gardener, John Raffald. They left the Hall in 1763 and moved from the pleasant countryside of Cheshire to the smoky, ever-growing centre of Manchester. Throughout her life, Elizabeth had nine children, three daughters of which survived infancy. Whilst continuously pregnant and starting a new chapter of her life at a time when most women would have expected to be in a comfortable and permanent position, Elizabeth was about to begin her life as an entrepreneur.

Illustration by **Laura Boast**

121

Elizabeth's business empire began not with her famous household and recipe book, but with a shop in Manchester that sold hot food, cakes and confectionary, that she opened upon her move to the city. It was from this shop that she ran her employment agency for reliable servants and would begin to release the Manchester Trade Directories in 1772. She ran an advertisement for these Directories, part of which read:

'…I have taken on the arduous task of compiling a complete guide for the easy finding out every Inhabitant of the least Consequence as also most of the County Tradesman; and the places where their warehouses are, likewise an account of the stage coaches and the carriers with times of their comings and goings out of town…'

To create the Manchester Directories was, as Elizabeth addresses in her advert, an incredibly challenging task; she herself claims that there are likely to be errors throughout. It offered the massively expanding Manchester, a place bustling with merchants, new businesses and new workers arriving to find employment, a way of navigating the city's trade. The success of Elizabeth's shop led to the opening of a second shop, where she was credited for selling high quality bridal and christening cakes. It was around this time that Elizabeth began to write the recipe book that would sit on the shelves of every respectable household.

The tenth print run of her book proudly included 'an engraved head of the author'. The portrait shows an elegantly dressed woman, a whole world away from the idea one might have of an 18th century cook. She holds a copy of her book, extending it out of the frame in an act of encouragement to the reader. The portrait shows Elizabeth at the height of her success.

The foreword of the book, written by Elizabeth herself. In it she states:

'I have made it my study to please both the eye and the palate, without using pernicious things for the sake of beauty…they will not be found very expensive, nor add compositions but as plain as the nature of the dish will admit of. The receipts for the confectionary as such that I daily sell in my own shop, which any Lady may examine at pleasure, as I still continue to best endeavours to give satisfaction to all who are pleased to favour me with their custom.'

She demonstrates a tenacity and a confidence that was key to her success. It is a book built on practice and whilst she admits there are many books like hers, she encourages her readers:

'...not to censure my work before they have made trial of some one receipt, which I am persuaded, if carefully followed, will answer their expectations...'

A declaration from the author herself that the proof is in the pudding. Elizabeth wasn't wrong; the book was a huge success. Queen Victoria copied passages into her diaries and the book ended up on the shelves of every respectable household in the country. It was a book written for all women, from the humble maid, to the prestigious housekeeper, to the lady of the house. It is a book dedicated to women – Elizabeth dedicates the volume to Lady Elizabeth Warburton, her former employer.

Elizabeth shows a powerful woman does not have to be a political woman. She was clever, keeping within the boundaries of domesticity, but making it a place for women, dictated by women.

Elizabeth died suddenly in 1781. Sadly, her successful role as head of the business was proven when her husband, an alcoholic, was unable to cope. Lacking any good business sense, he racked up huge debts, putting an end to Elizabeth's legacy.

Or so it might have seemed. After her death, Elizabeth's book went on to be published more than three times, both in the United Kingdom and it was subsequently adapted for American audiences. She is memorialised by a plaque in Manchester City Centre and some of her recipes are still being made today.

EMILY WILLIAMSON

There is often an assumption that Victorian and early Edwardian women, if passionate about a cause, only fought for one: the vote. But some of the most prolific campaigners in the late 19th and early 20th century campaigned not solely for social issues, but for an issue that still occupies international debate and action today – the conservation and preservation of nature and wildlife. Women, particularly those from wealthy backgrounds, were expected to have a charitable output, and women such as Octavia Hill, one of the founders of the National Trust, and Beatrix Potter, author and conservationist, are the reason that so much green space and wild species has survived over the last two hundred years. By today's standards this may be considered as 'gentle' activism – particularly compared to the militant actions of the suffragettes that occurred alongside - but it would have taken guts and tenacity to undertake such a huge challenge.

One of the biggest conservation charities today is the Royal Society for the Protection of Birds (RSPB). It has over a million members and carries out incredible work for wildlife protection in the UK. It is little-known that the RSPB was founded in Fletcher Moss Park by a quiet, diligent and dedicated Victorian woman, Emily Williamson.

Emily was born on 17th April 1855 to Frederick and Eliza Bateson, in Lancaster. Little is known of her childhood, but she was raised in a middle-class household and in June 1882 she married Robert Williamson. Robert's father had been a professor at Owen's College in Manchester, where Robert had inherited his

love of anthropology and botany – something that would fill the home of the Williamsons at The Croft in Didsbury. At the time, Didsbury was a wealthy suburb of the city and the Williamsons would have settled into the quietly respectful area nicely. Their home was large and elegant, surrounded with beautifully crafted gardens. Didsbury would have felt like a world away from the radical happenings in Manchester. Towards the end of the 19th century and the start of the 20th, the city centre was filled with meetings, debates and discussions around questions of everything from workers rights to women's suffrage. Societies for women were starting to flourish and women were becoming undeterred, unafraid to have a say. Even in her sleepy, elegant garden in Didsbury, Emily felt the tremors of this and would soon begin to fight against the deplorable plumage trade.

In the late Victorian era, walking down any fashionable street in Manchester would have been a maze of bustling dresses and fabulously decorated hats. Feathers were imported from across the British Empire to supply the milliners of England. They accessorised almost every hat in the country and some even used the entire bird. What many of the ladies who donned these hats didn't know was the methods that were used to collect the feathers they adorned themselves with. Entire species were depleted as hundreds of thousands of birds were killed in the plumage trade, a trade that had been made all too lucrative due to the Industrial Revolution. The plumage trade, in the late 1800s, seemed indestructible.

Illustration by **Sarah Wilson**

In Manchester, the city famous for its textile industry and home to many a millinery, an eyelid had barely been batted to this ruthless trade, that was based purely on vanity. The city had been somewhat preoccupied, with the fight for reform and the demand for suffrage. Indeed, when Emily Williamson moved to Manchester in the early 1880s, the city had cemented its reputation as the most radical city in the country.

Although we may never know what Emily thought of the campaign for reform – particularly the rising demand across the city for votes for women – it was an act of shameless inequality that led to her forming the Plumage Society at The Croft in Didsbury. It is unsurprising that Emily had a prior interest in bird life. The surrounding trees of Fletcher Moss Park must have been full of feathers and bird song, plenty for Emily to observe from the windows of the Croft or whilst walking in the gardens. As the wife of a successful solicitor, who in addition had inherited some of the family fortune, Emily was not required to work and therefore could give more of her time to both charitable and leisurely pursuits.

Emily had attempted to give her time to help save the birds already, but found herself rebuffed. She had tried to join the British Ornithologists' Union, but like many societies at the time, it barred women from joining. Therefore, in February 1889, determined to do something, she formed her own society in the living rooms of The Croft. The society had a relaxed view towards organising at first; it cost two pennies to join, but there were no requirements for joining except one – men were not allowed. The Society for the Protection of Birds (SPB) pledged that they would *'discourage the wanton destruction of birds and interest themselves generally in their protection'* and *'refrain from wearing the feathers of any bird not killed for purposes of food, the ostrich only excepted.'* Ostrich feathers could be acquired without killing the bird.

The society grew more quickly than perhaps Emily expected. In her small suburb in Manchester, Emily was making a difference. Emily advertised the society and its endeavours in local newspapers and gained support from naturalists and journalists; soon, the SPB were known nationwide. There began to be wide-spread recognition of their resistance from highly-regarded conservationists and naturalists. The very society that had barred Emily in the first place now expressed their support for the SPB. Lord Lilford, President of the British Ornithologists' Union wrote:

'…I am delighted to believe that in this country at least a very considerable check has been put upon this atrocious business by the action of the ladies' 'Society for the Protection of Birds,' an association that cannot be too widely made known, or too highly commended. I would strongly urge all ladies who may honour me by reading these notes, to enroll themselves as members of this really beneficent society, whose only object is the preservation from wanton destruction of some of the most interesting and beautiful of organised creatures…'

Emily and the women of Manchester were not alone in their resistance. In Croydon, an almost identical group of ladies led by Eliza Phillips and Etta Lemon had formed; the Fur, Fin and Feather Folk Society, which had similar aims as the RSPB. Emily corresponded with the group and in 1891, the two groups formed under one name, creating a widespread, national movement that continued to agitate for change. Lady Sutherland became the president of the society and they opened offices in London, from which they sent everything from newsletters, essays and even Christmas cards to their members. In 1904, the society was given Royal Charter, after only fifteen years since its foundation. Emily was recorded as saying at the Annual General Meeting that year, that she had founded the SPB:

'…when it was a very small fledgling, and had no dreams of soaring to the heights which it had reached…'

Emily remained heavily involved in the SPB, although was perhaps not the leading voice. She continued to run the Manchester branch until 1911, combining it with her other charitable work, including founding the Gentlewoman's Employment Association. Her commitment to supporting women in higher education and training continued until she left the city and moved to the south east. Both in London and in Surrey, Emily stayed committed to local branches of the SPB, remaining active in the running of the organisations. She passed away on 12th October 1936. In her obituary, the Manchester Guardian summarised her quiet but committed life succinctly:

'…many who never knew her knew of her as the originator behind these valuable institutions…which were first laid down through her energy, her practical sense, and her inspiring personality.'

Nature conservation is more important today than ever. Emily isn't Emmeline Pankhurst. She did not shout loud, nor gather crowds of thousands of people - she was barely ever divisive. But the legacy Emily leaves behind is this: one person committing to make a change is no small action. She proved that by asking others to help make that change, a cause could spread. Soon, what is considered an outside belief, becomes a universal acceptance of what needs to change and what us, as humans, can do to make that happen. Without Emily and Etta, the protection of birds and the conservation of natural habitats may never have happened at the pace that it did.

SUNNY LOWRY

The history of Manchester's radical and revolutionary past stems from the industrial roots of the city. The worker bees in the hive of industry created a prosperous city and it's no surprise that the architecture reflects it. Victoria Baths, a water palace for bathing and swimming, was a jewel for workers and middle classes alike. Although men and women and people from different class backgrounds were kept separate, Victoria Baths – or Hathersage Baths, as it was commonly known – was a place for the people of Manchester to bathe, swim and socialise up until its closure in 1993.

A stained-glass window now installed in Victoria Baths commemorates perhaps the most famous woman who swam in the pools there. Ethel 'Sunny' Lowry defied sexism in sport to become one of the most celebrated female swimmers of the 20th century. In 1933, Sunny made headlines across the country when she swam English Channel. Sunny had started her swimming career in Manchester and fell in love with the sport whilst training in the pools of Victoria Baths. A tenacious and determined woman, Sunny didn't let failure stand in the way of her goals and didn't give up on her dream of swimming the Channel, even when it felt impossible.

For a long time Sunny insisted that she was the first woman to swim the Channel. We now know this to be false. She also claimed to be a second cousin of the renowned Salford artist, L.S Lowry, but again, there is no evidence to suggest that the two were related. Although Sunny was in fact the fifth woman to swim the Channel, it by no means dampens her victory, or the celebration she brought to Manchester with such an achievement.

Sunny was born Ethel Lowry on 2nd January 1911, to William and Elizabeth Lowry. William was a fish seller at the Manchester fish market and Ethel, or Sunny as she was nicknamed, was raised with her four brothers and sisters in a spacious but crowded house on Kirkmanshulme Lane, Levenshulme. Sunny attended Manchester High School for Girls, famous alumni of which had been the Pankhurst sisters some twenty years earlier. Sunny was a strong-willed student who knew what her goal would be; as she recalled later in life, when the headmistress asked what she wanted to achieve, she replied staunchly:

'Swim the Channel.'

The headmistress immediately dismissed her, but she was not deterred. As part of the Levenshulme Swimming Club, she began swimming frequently at Victoria Baths, before joining the Victoria Ladies Swimming Club. She began to go on outdoor swims, out of the city and into the Lake District.

Illustration by **Eve Warren**

129

Sunny knew from a young age that she would swim the Channel, so swim the Channel she would. In 1932, she began her journey towards fulfilling her dream. Beating three hundred other young women who had applied for the same place, Sunny won a coveted position to train with Jabez Wolffe, a Channel swimming instructor who was renowned for training champions. The advert read:

'Wanted – a British-born girl aged 17 to 20, weight about 11 stone, with the courage to beat Captain Webb's channel swimming time of 21 ¾ hours.'

Jabez was a Glaswegian who had tried, and failed, to swim the Channel more than twenty times since 1911, on several occasions falling at the final hurdle in the last few hundred yards. Jabez had trained previous women including Hilda Sharp and Peggy Duncan. When he had attempted to swim the Channel, he had adopted unorthodox methods including having bagpipes play in the tugboat alongside him to keep him in a better rhythm. Jabez did not adopt these tactics with Sunny but did warn her when she began training with him in Kent and Dover, that if she complained about the cold water she might as well give up now. Sunny later recalled that she would often leave the sea unable to feel her ankles.

Under the guidance of Jabez, Sunny was on course to achieve her dream. She travelled down to Brighton to train with him and on 19th August 1932, she made her first attempt at the swim, from England to France. In preparation for her attempts, Sunny ate forty eggs a week and built up a rigorous training routine, increasing her weight to fourteen stone to factor in the weight she would lose whilst swimming. Nature apprehended her first try, as the strong currents proved too much for her after fourteen hours in the water. Later in life, Sunny would recall this first attempt fondly, as she swam alongside dolphins and would later name her long-distance swimming club after her first channel companions. Her second attempt on 27th July 1933 also ended after only six hours due to bad luck and circumstances out of her control; in the early hours of the morning, a storm broke out. The pilot boat took almost an hour to recall Sunny from the water, only spotting her when the searchlight fell on her red swimming cap.

Only a month later, Sunny was ready to try again. She left at 6.36pm on 28th August 1933, from Gris Nez in France. The log of her swim shows the signatures of those who witnessed the swim, testifying she had swam it alone and without assistance. The signatories include Jabez and her mother Elizabeth. Accompanied by her pilot boat, *Isabelle*, Sunny stopped on occasion to drink some beef tea and coffee.

As had once happened with Jabez, a piper played on board *Isabelle*, keeping pace and rhythm with her. This time, the weather didn't intervene and Sunny arrived, after fifteen hours and forty-one minutes, in the water at St Margaret's Bay at 10.17am on 29th August. She didn't walk, but crawled up the beach covered in jellyfish stings and sporting blue lips from the cold. Exhausted and in pain, it was still a moment of exhilaration and relief: she had realised her dream and had swam the English Channel.

Accompanying Sunny on her journey was her pilot's flag, that she was later photographed waving victoriously as well as standing in front of. Sunny had made the flag herself to fly on the boat that accompanied her on her victorious swim. The emblem in the centre of the banner was the worker bee, the symbol of Manchester, flanked by the Union Jack flag and the red rose of Lancashire. The letters LSC – for Levenshulme Swimming Club - were embroidered above the bee and 'Manchester' was embroidered below.

The banner represented her pride in her hometown, where she had learnt to love swimming and where her dream had been thought up.

Sunny became an instant celebrity and was welcomed back to Manchester with a roaring fanfare. However, her victory was somewhat slighted; whilst most male swimmers would not have been questioned or reproached after such a victory, Sunny was attacked by several members of the press for her swimming costume. Considered incredibly risqué at the time, Sunny had worn a crimson two-piece swimsuit; for such a long and gruelling swim, the suit would have breathed easier and not become weighed down, unlike the older, woollen styles she would have been expected to wear. For bearing her knees, Sunny was dismissed as uncouth and branded a harlot. The scandalous costume is now on display at the Dover Museum.

Still, this did not dampen Sunny's success. She was accoladed across the professional swimming world, opened new baths and carried out demonstrations at galas and later in life turned to teaching and coaching, sometimes alongside her husband William Anderson. She became the president of the Channel Swimming Association in 2000.

Sunny never forgot Victoria Baths and advocated for its restoration in 2003, acting as an incredible and influential campaigner. Her love for her city is visible in everything she did and her determination for swimming to be open and accessible to all shaped the current of her life. She passed away on 21st February 2008, months before the baths re-opened, remaining active, energetic and sharp until the very end.

'Rise up women, for the fight is hard'

On Friday 14th December 2018, one hundred years to the day since some women first voted in a general election, the unveiling of Emmeline's statue took place in St Peter's Square.

Early on the crowd started to build. Hosted by BBC's Naga Munchetty, there were cameras and journalists jostling to the front of the crowd to capture this iconic moment in history. In attendance were representatives from Greater Manchester's ten local authorities, including Sir Richard Leese, and Greater Manchester Mayor Andy Burnham was also present. The entire county, it felt, was there to mark the commemoration of a woman who, over a century ago, was considered the biggest thorn in the side of authority. Over six thousand people were viewing the event from every vantage point, with two big screens relaying proceedings to those at the back of the crowd. A key element in the design of the statue is accessibility. In the front row of the crowd were two women in wheelchairs and nine service users from Henshaws Society for Blind People, two with their guide dogs. Nobody was excluded from this historic moment.

In a sea of purple, white and green, the marchers from the Pankhurst Centre and People's History Museum poured into the square. You heard them before you saw them, singing and chanting the songs that would have been heard in the city centuries ago. Helen Pankhurst and Hazel Reeves lead the marches, their WSPU sashes prevalent, to the place in St Peter's Square where a bulk of purple satin covered Hazel's

sculpture. Emmeline had arrived, and the crowd were waiting with anticipation. The scene wasn't dissimilar from one seen a hundred years ago, when Emmeline, risen on a platform for all to see, would have appeared with resonating words demanding equality, demanding freedom and fairness. Now, there were no police lurking to fight their way to the dias to arrest her. Now, her female bodyguards trained to help her escape from the arms of the law were no longer surrounding her. The mix of anticipation and determination with the tension of arrest, of brutality, was gone. There would be no fight for Emmeline that day.

It began with a moment that could have stirred the soul of the gathered crowds. Directed and performed by Liz Power, the Manchester Community Choir sang Nana Was a Suffragette. It was a reminder of all the other women, ordinary women, who played their part in this giant movement, this shaking of shackles, this cry for equality. The lyrics don't speak of the Pankhursts, but of what happened afterwards:

'The proudest day in Nana's life
was when the vote was won
The papers said "It's over!"
but Nan had just begun
Her Women's Committee went on to better things
And they challenged the Union, the Council
and their wedding rings ...'

When the crowd stopped applauding, a hush descended as the proceedings began. The silence was only ever interrupted with rousing cheers for the powerful speeches, from Andrew Simcock, Helen Pankhurst, Fatima Shahid, Sarah Judge and Baroness Williams, Equality Minister in the House of Lords.

The moment soon came that everybody had been waiting for. Every woman who had spoken took a handful of the purple cloth and a deafening cheer filled the square as it fell away to reveal Rise Up Women. Emmeline is stood on an ordinary kitchen chair, hand stretched out towards the crowd, her Holloway brooch pinned to her collar. She is mid-speech, and it is up to each member of the crowd to imagine what she might be saying. A message of hope? A message of defiance? Of peace or war? Is this a cry to smash windows, or a cry to march? Is she addressing a hostile crowd, or an enraptured one? Is there a person in the crowd, afraid, unsure to take up action? Is this the speech that will rouse them to take up arms for the fight? It could be any of these, but the message carved into the base summarises them all.

Rise Up Women.

Hazel Reeves made the final speech. The crowds stretched out their arms at her instruction, copying Emmeline. There, in the final moments of the event, was Emmeline's greatest legacy. Thousands of people copying her actions. Thousands of women, from young school children to older activists, pledging to take up her fight. Afterwards, crowds swarmed to Emmeline, taking photographs and examining the exquisite details of the statue up close. It was the closing ceremony that the year of the centenary deserved.

And so, Emmeline's statue stands in the centre of the city for all to see. The fight for representation however, is not over. There are so many more fights; fights started by the twenty women in this book, fights that need more than a placard or march, fights that need to be taken to the highest powers and fights that are happening internationally.

There's no shame in exhaustion, in the feeling that a fight is lost, or that, once won, it is time to sit down leaving others to carry on their own battles. But what this list shows – this minute selection of the power women create and hold in this city - is that one voice is only the start of a fight and never the end. When we speak together, and loudly, that is when the fight is won. Emmeline Pankhurst would never have become the prominent figure she today without scores of suffragists and suffragettes across the nation and, of course, across Manchester, who supported the movement.

There are many ways to remember the other nineteen women on this list. In our deeds and in our words. When we walk past or turn away from injustice, inequality and intolerance, we should think of Margaret Ashton, of Louise Da-Cocodia, of Ellen Wilkinson, and act like they did. We can still be angry. We can still create action and every bit of action we create, every fight we win, every step closer we inch towards equality, we make it easier for those to come, for the women who will take over from us the same way we have taken over from the twenty women on this list.

It is best to sign off with the words of Emmeline Pankhurst herself.

'If we win it, this hardest of all fights, then, to be sure, in the future it is going to be made easier for women all over the world to win their fight when their time comes.'

SELECTED BIBLIOGRAPHY

The author would like to express special thanks and gratitude to Warp & Weft and Ali Ronan for providing insight into the lives of many of the twenty women

Margaret Downes
- Bush, M.J (2007) *Casualties of Peterloo*, Carnegie Publishing Ltd
- Mather, R (2014) '*These Lancashire women are witches in politics*': Female reform societies and the theatre of radicalism, 1819–1820: Return to Peterloo, (Manchester Region History Review), vol.23, 2012
- Riding, J (2018) *Peterloo: The Story of the Massacre*, Apollo Publishing

Margaret Ashton
- Cowman, K (2010), *Women in British Politics, C.1689-1979*, Palgrave Macmillan
- Crawford, E (2000), *The Women's Suffrage Movement: A Reference Guide 1866-1928*, Routledge

Mary Quaile
- Hyland, B, Herbert, M (2016) *Dare to Be Free: Women in Trade Unions, Past and Present*, Mary Quaile Club

Ellen Wilkinson
- Bartley, P (2014) *Ellen Wilkinson: From Red Suffragist to Government Minister*, Pluto Press
- Beers, L (2016) *Red Ellen: The Life of Ellen Wilkinson, Socialist, Feminist, Internationalist*, University of Harvard Press
- Perry, M (2015) *'Red Ellen' Wilkinson: Her Ideas, Movements and the World*, University of Manchester Press
- Vernon, B (1982) Ellen Wilkinson: A Biography, Croom Helm

Esther Roper
- Tiernan, S (2012) *Eva Gore-Booth: An Image of Such Politics*, University of Manchester Press

Lydia Becker
- Crawford, E (2006) *The Women's Suffrage Movement in Britain and Ireland: A Regional Survey*, Routledge
- Liddington, J, Norris, J (2000) *One Hand Tied Behind Us (revised ed.)*, Rivers Oram Press

Christabel, Emmeline and Sylvia Pankhurst
- Connelly, K (2015) *Sylvia Pankhurst: Suffragette, Socialist and Scourge of Empire*, Pluto Press
- Pankhurst, E (1914), *My Own Story*
- Pankhurst, E.S, (1911) *The Suffragette*
- Pankhurst, E.S, (1931) *The Suffragette Movement*
- Pugh, M, (2009) *The Pankhursts*, Vintage
- Purvis, J (2003) *Emmeline Pankhurst: A Biography*, Routledge
- Purvis, J (2018) *Christabel Pankhurst: A Biography*, Routledge

Annie Horniman
- Fraizer, A (1992) *Behind the Scenes: Yeats, Horniman, and the Struggle for the Abbey Theatre*, University of California Press
- Goddie, S (2013) *Annie Horniman: A Pioneer in Theatre.* Albert Bridge Books

Elizabeth Raffald

• Appleton, S (2015) *Elizabeth Raffald: The Experienced English Housekeeper of Manchester*, CreateSpace Independent Publishing
• Appleton, S (2015) *The Manchester Directories 1772, 1773 & 1781 by Elizabeth Raffald*, CreateSpace Independent Publishing

Emily Williamson

• Boase, T (2018) *Mrs Pankhurst's Purple Feather: A scandalous history of birds, hats and votes*, Aurum Press Ltd

Enriqueta Rylands

• Farnie, D.A, (1993) *John Rylands of Manchester*, John Rylands University Library of Manchester

Olive Shapley

• Shapley, O (1996) *Broadcasting: A Life, Scarlet Press*

Kathleen Ollerenshaw

• Ollerenshaw, K, Moore, P (2004) *To Talk of Many Things: An Autobiography*, Manchester University Press

Marie Stopes

• Debenham, C (2018) *Marie Stopes' Sexual Revolution and the Birth Control Movement*, Palgrave Pivot Publishing

Elizabeth Gaskell

• Chapple, J.V, Pollard, A (1997) *The Letters of Mrs Gaskell*, Manchester University Press
• Chapple, J (1997) *Elizabeth Gaskell: The Early Years*, Manchester University Press

Shena Simon

• Goodman, J, Martin, J (2004) *Women in Education, 1800 – 1980*, Pangrave Macmillan

Louise Da-Cocodia

• For information on Louise Da-Cocodia please visit the Louise Da-Cocodia Education Trust website, http://dacocodiatrust.com/

WOMEN IN PRINT

On an unexpectedly hot evening in July 2016, in a corner of Ancoats, Women in Print held the private view of its first exhibition. This was a collection of sixteen individual prints by local creatives visually interpreting the lives and achievements of iconic women from Greater Manchester. In attendance were councillor and Womanchester Statue Project founder Andrew Simcock, Dr Helen Pankhurst and some of the sculptors who had shown interest in the (then to be conceived) Emmeline Pankhurst statue.

Since that evening, both Women in Print and the Womanchester Statue Project have supported one another. Our projects have grown and become part of a wider, feminist movement in Manchester that is fighting for equal opportunities and better representation of women within public spaces.

First in the Fight felt like a natural partnership for our two projects. The book cements the legacy of Manchester's first female statue in 100 years and furthers Women in Print's mission to champion female creativity. This book not only brings to life the stories of twenty incredible women, it also showcases the tremendous creative, female talent we have working in the north of England.

From art to political reform, the deeds and words of women from Manchester and the neighbouring towns which make up Greater Manchester, have shaped the world we live in today. This hasn't always been fairly represented in the printed pages of history. Their achievements are invisible threads woven into the fabric of Manchester's success.

Women in Print aims to shine a light on women's history and the stories within our places through print by working with a broad range of artists, designers, illustrators and makers. It's founder, designer Jane Bowyer, started the project because she was angry at what she regarded as the lazy, two-dimensional stereotyping of women in printed magazines, newspapers and advertisements. Women in Print became an opportunity to challenge the way women were being portrayed in print and foster a collaborative community of creative women in Manchester.

Over the last three years Women in Print has delivered an artistic programme of exhibitions, events and commissions across the Greater Manchester and beyond. Its aim is to deliver socially thought-provoking work on gender equality and inspire an appreciation and recognition of all creative arts, not just those traditionally valued as higher art but those arts rooted in traditional 'domestic' crafts.

Women in Print is proud to have supported local charities Manchester Women's Aid and Smart Works Great Manchester through donations made from the sale of prints. It is also proud to support The Monthly Gift, a grassroots organisation campaigning to end period poverty in Greater Manchester, by accepting donations of sanitary care products at events.

Many thanks to those who have engaged with the project, attended our events and have seen and understood the value of the work of women. Finally, a thank-you to the talented artists included in this book: Alex Francis, Amy Rochester, Artsynibs, Chelsea Waites, Deanna Halsall, Ellie Thomas, Emily Dayson, Emma Bowen, Eve Warren, Halah El-Kholy, Helen Musselwhite, Laura Boast, Laura Bohill, Maisy Summer, Nell Smith, Nicola Fernandes, Sarah Wilson, Sneaky Racoon, Tomekah George, Wendy Wong and all the artists we have worked with to date.

METROLINK

Metrolink services continued running through St Peter's Square on Friday when around 2,500 people gathered for the unveiling of a statue of Emmeline Pankhurst.

Weeks of preparations mean trams were able to move through the square at the same time the event took place on the penultimate Friday before Christmas, and possibly one of the busiest days of the year for people travelling across Greater Manchester.

During planning, the team from Metrolink and Emmeline Pankhurst Statue Committee recreated the iconic 1908 picture of Emmeline obstructing a tram in Heaton Park with fellow protestors – part of the suffrage movement that achieved equal voting rights for women.

The unveiling of the statue took place during a programme of events in St Peter's Square between 11am and 1.30pm on Friday 14 December, which was 100 years to the day since women voted for the first time.

Aline Frantzen, Managing Director at KeolisAmey Metrolink (KAM), said: *"Times have changed for the better in the last 100 years so there was no need for Emmeline to stop the trams on this occasion!*

"It was vital we helped mark this occasion and, at the same time, run the best service possible on what was one of the busiest days on the network in 2018, with many out shopping and celebrating the festive season.

"By doing this, KAM delivered on its commitment to keep Greater Manchester moving every day and continually improve how we manage large events that affect the whole city-region.

"We paused services at the most poignant times of the unveiling ceremony to minimise any disruption to our customers –

otherwise trams were guided through by our teams on the ground at slower than usual speeds and allowed our customers to be part of the event, extending its reach to those who might not otherwise have seen it.

"As a woman leading delivery of a key part of Greater Manchester's recent history – Metrolink – it was of great personal and professional pride to be a positive part of this wonderful occasion.

"It was equally important to ensure we played a part in this book and supported the recording of the history of all the women who were on the shortlist to be commemorated via the statue in St Peter's Square, and create a legacy for the future through telling the stories of all these women who have a significance to Manchester."

Measures in place to enable the ceremony to go ahead included:
• Trams travelling at slower speeds through St Peter's Square throughout the event.
• Barriers to ensure the crowds attending do not stray onto the track.
• Metrolink staff on duty on the St Peter's Square platforms and around the square to guide people and trams safely through.
• Trams did not use their street horns in the square throughout the event.
• Platform announcements and external tram announcements were not be made between 12pm and 1pm.
• Trams held outside the square for two short periods (one of four minutes and one of five minutes) between 12.15pm and 12.45pm.

These measures minimised disruption and, while there were some delays, it meant that Metrolink did not have to run replacement buses on what was also a busy day on the roads.

Bridget Aherne
Head of Communications

WEIGHTMANS

When I was first approached to help with an exciting new project showcasing some of Manchester's most influential women, I never expected to be writing for a book, a piece of history dedicated to this initiative, captured for years to come.

This project was about celebrating the significant role that women have played in the evolution of Manchester - it has been incredible to learn more about these twenty trailblazers, these women who fought for social change and equality, who made huge sacrifices to secure a future for the next generation that is fair and safe.

After the voting took place and Emmeline Pankhurst was chosen, I agreed to undertake legal work related to the statue completely pro bono, working on legal agreements relating to the sculpture and being available to Andrew and his team for any advice or support. I am a partner at Weightmans and have been with the firm since I was a trainee, rising through the ranks. Weightmans is a national law firm, with an office in Spinningfields, Manchester, providing a complete range of legal services to businesses and individuals. Whether through pro bono support, fundraising or volunteering, we are proud of our thriving CSR programme and commitment to social mobility and equality.

Emmeline and the suffrage movement ensured a vital cultural and political change towards the equal rights we all benefit from today and I am so proud to have played my part in bringing the first female monument in over a century to the city.

This project was about celebrating the significant role that women have played in the evolution of Manchester and I am delighted to have been approached to provide legal advice to make the first female monument in Manchester in over 100 years a reality - it has been a great project to be involved in and the final result is truly inspiring.

I hope you'll agree that this book is a true celebration of a woman's role in making Manchester the great city it is - a fitting tribute to the project, to these fantastic women and to the hard work of everyone who made it possible, which will continue to motivate, educate and encourage us all.

Sarah Walton
Partner at Weightmans

FRIENDS OF 'OUR EMMELINE'

Michele Abendstern
Paul Allen
Catherine Antrobus
Derek Antrobus
Deborah Bailey
Sheila Barker
Dianne Bell
Tori Blakeman
Laura Boast
Gill Bradley
Kathy Brooks
Ellie Buck
Tracey Bucknell
Christine Bullock
Paul Burns
Gwen Cameron
Jessica Campbell
Christine Caudwell
William Clarke
Marie Collier
Hefina Jayne Cookson
Susan Cooley
Sarah Cowan
Eloise Victoria Crawshaw
Jayne Alexandra Crawshaw
Elizabeth Cresswell
Lyn Davies
Angela Davies
Jeff Dawson
Christine Dawson
Gaywin Dayson
Bill Dayson

Karen De Vine
Bernadette Delaney
Caroline Edwards
Khadija Ehsan
Joanne Ellis
Joanne. T. Faux
Sarah Fern
Helen Fisher
Susan Frost
Victoria Frow
Paul Gilmour
David Godfrey
Mandie Shilton Godwin
Sue Good
Charlotte Green
Jennifer Harvey
Meghan Healy
Manchester High School For Girls
Kerima Hill
Hilda Holland
Helen Jackson
Karin Janzon
Esther Lisk-Carew
Kris MacNaughton
Sandra Martin
Gemma McCall
Lesley McCarthy
Alison McDade
Kirsty-May McKie
Sarah Miller
Tommy Miller
Harriet Monkhouse

Dennis Morgan
Caroline Morris
Ann Moulton
Nigel Murphy
Diane Murphy
Nadia Nadarajah
Sue Northeast
Sian Odgers
Helen Oxley
Linsey Parkinson
Hilary Peate
Suzannah Reeves
Suzanne Richards
Margaret Seaby
Heather Self
Helen Elizabeth Shaw
Roberta Spagnul
Joan Summers
Imogen Thompson
Larraine Thompson
Lian Trowers
Dawn Waites
Chelsea Waites
Moire Walker
Kaleigh Watterson
E Webster
Gavin White
Manda Whitehead
Theresa Wilkie
Edwina Wolstencroft
David Woods
Barbara Young

Acknowledgements

Ian 'Tom' Tomie for providing the
'Dartmoor in the fog' photo

Official Event Photographers : Emma Finch,
Sue Anders, Nigel Kingston, Karen Wright,
Bernadette Delaney, Andrew Simcock

The WoManchester Statue Campaign: many
more photographs, video and other material
relating to the statue project and the unveiling
can be found at www.womanchesterstatue.org
and on Twitter @ouremmeline

To my co-author Andrew and the team at
iNostalgia, thank you for your incredibly hard
work publishing this book and bringing it to life.
Emily – you've been a wonderful editor and thank
you so much for all your support and help.

To Jane Bowyer, a woman of such incredible
talent and brilliance. To work with you
and to see your vision unfold has been
a joy. Your commitment and passion for
the past, present and future of women's
activism has been an inspiration.

To Jon – thank you for putting up with the
tapping of the keyboard late into the night, for
all the food, all the motivation, the patience.
'Faithful and true and my ever-loving comrade'

To my parents. Every lesson of courage, love,
resilience, kindness and encouragement comes
from you both. Thank you for everything.

To my sisters. I'm fortunate that you are more
loving, loyal and caring than the Pankhurst sisters
were to each other. Lucy, Jen, and Catherine -
there is nobody in the world who has influenced
and encouraged me like you, and I would be lost
without you.

I am surrounded by a host of immensely
incredible, bold, talented, hilarious women, and
without them cheering me on, this book wouldn't
have come to fruition: Jane, Grace, Steph,
Elizabeth, Clare, Laura, Jemma, Charlie, Jodie,
Samantha, Natasha.
We shouldn't always look up to women in
history for strength and inspiration, but
to those who stand at our sides. Together,
we go forward, and carry on the fight.

To the team at People's History Museum
(especially the team in TCS, Jenny and
Kloe!) thank you for the constant support
and for allowing us to share the remarkable
story of the First in the Fight banner.

This book would not have been possible without
a host of historians, academics and curators,
whose research, knowledge and insight have
been invaluable. Across this city, across this
country, there is a strong network getting these
stories told, unearthing what has previously
been hidden, and bringing women's history
to the forefront. Long may it continue.